Erie REFLECTIONS

Volume Two

Published by

Erie Times-News
Times Publishing Company
Erie, Pennsylvania

Printed by:
Heeter Printing Company

Cover Photo:
1913 Niagara
The U.S. Brig Niagara is shown in Lake Erie in this 1913 photo following the restoration of the ship.

In 1913, the sunken remains of Niagara were raised from her grave at the bottom of Misery Bay. Using some of the original structure, the Niagara was reconstructed and towed by the Wolverine to Put-In-Bay for the 100th anniversary of the Battle of Lake Erie. *(Photo courtesy of the Erie Maritime Museum).*

FOREWORD

Quick – what is your most cherished possession? Most would say that family photos are at the top of the list.

Photographs are tangible evidence of our past – documented proof of where we've been and how far we've come. They are priceless, irreplaceable and fascinating. But, most importantly, photographs allow us to remember our friends and family and the moments that we shared with them.

In that spirit, I've included (at right) a poem entitled "Remember Me" written by Joseph Reilly, a poet and artist who lived in the Erie area at the turn of the 20th century. Joseph's descendants still live in the area and were generous enough to share this poem with us. It seemed especially fitting for this book which is all about remembering and reflecting on our past.

Once again, we hope you enjoy this reflection on the life and times of generations of Erie area residents. We thank all our Erie Times-News readers who shared their personal stories and photographs with us.

Heather Cass
Project Director

REMEMBER ME
by Joseph Reilly

In the quiet evening of your life,
Remember me.
And when the shadows fall,
Recall, just once again,
Those happy times, from long ago.
Let memory unfold,
Those wonder tales of old,
And dream again,
Those dreams of happiness,
Perhaps, fulfilled
And when you conjure up
These fantasies
From out the golden past,
I trust that in the last,
You'll find one little place
For me.

(Submitted by Mary Ann Granahan, Joseph's great-great niece).

ACKNOWLEDGEMENTS
Erie Reflections, Vol. II

Project Staff

Heather Cass, *Project Director*
Lisa Shade, *Cover Design/Promotions*
Rebecca Reese, *Photo Scanner*
Matt Madurski, *Caption Headlines*
Jeff Pinski, *Caption Editor*
Elizabeth Swantek, *Production Supervisor*
Sheila Coon, *Market Development Director*

Special Thanks

Connie Gibbs, Telegraph Herald
Mary Temple, Visiting Nurse Association
Gennifer Biggs, Mercyhurst College
Ed Blaguszewski, Penn State Erie, the Behrend College
Scott Mitchell, Erie Zoological Society
Robert Cross
All of our wonderful Erie Times-News readers who submitted photos

Parade Street Hardware

Shown in this 1890s photo is Theodore Ohmer's hardware store which was located at 27th and Parade streets in Erie. Theodore, a native of Germany, was also a well-known restaurant proprietor and also owned a place called "The Saloon" on the corner of 28th and Parade streets (where Herman's now stands). The men in this photo are unidentified, but one of them is likely Ohmer. Notice the condition of Parade Street (dirt road) and the horse hitches in front of the building. Theodore was married to Apollonia and they had nine children. (*Submitted by Bette Williams, great-granddaughter of Theodore Ohmer*).

Quick change

Jake and Freda Franz pose with their daughters, Freda and Emma, in this 1890s snapshot in front of their business – Jake's Bathhouse at Waldameer Beach (note the family dog who looks perfectly posed complete with a stick in his mouth). The Franz's offered men's and women's dressing rooms for beachgoers to change and store their clothes while swimming in the lake. According to the contributor, Erie visitors would take a trolley to the foot of Peninsula Drive (for five cents) and walk down to the bathhouse from there. They would then pay 25 cents to rent a "house" to change in and to lock up their clothes while swimming. By 1910, Jake's Bathhouse had 110 men's dressing rooms and 79 women's dressing rooms. In the photo below, swimmers are shown frolicking in the water near Jake's Bathhouse in 1910. They had two swings that visitors would use to catapult into the water. Bathhouse owner, Jake Franz, is on the pier in the left side of the photo in the white shirt. *(Submitted by Patricia Surrena, granddaughter of Jake and Freda Franz).*

Where's the fire?

A group of Erie firefighters pose in front of Fire Station #6 at 18th and Liberty Streets in this c. 1890s photo. The men are: Dan Coughlin, George Anderson, Michael Cronin, Maurice Murray and Martin Cribbins. *(Courtesy of the Firefighters Historical Museum Inc.).*

Village Crossroads

The Tuttle School House in Harborcreek (above) was located on Station Road (near Kuhl Road) and was torn down in 1959 due to the construction of Interstate 90. From the very beginning, Harborcreek Township contained three villages — Wesleyville, Harborcreek and Mooreheadville. Each of these villages, all located on Buffalo Road, were stopover points on the stagecoach line between Erie and New York state. Later, when the railroad and trolley lines were laid these villages became major stations along their routes. They also became the site of official post offices of the township. Wesleyville was incorporated as a separate borough in 1912.
(Donated to Harborcreek Historical Society by Robert W. Tuttle).

First ladies

Elizabeth McGowen (first row, third from left), the Loyal Christian Benefit Association's (LCBA) first president, served from 1890 to 1910. She is shown here with her National Board of Trustees in 1890. The LCBA was established in 1890 in Titusville, Pa., as the Ladies Catholic Benevolent Association to provide life insurance for women at a time when only men were deemed worthy of insurance. The LCBA, originally operated by and for women only, opened its membership in 1960 to all Christian men, women and children and changed its name to the current Loyal Christian Benefit Association. *(Submitted by the LCBA).*

Blacksmith open for business

H.D. Hovis' blacksmith shop, located on the corner of Third and Chestnut streets in Waterford, is shown in these interior and exterior shots believed to have been taken in the mid 1800s. The blacksmith shop is now a personal residence in Waterford. *(Submitted by Anita Palmer, great-granddaughter of H.D. Hovis).*

Players give tacklers the slip

This c. 1898 photo shows a much different type of football team. According to the photo contributor, Kenneth Massing, the men in leather vests were backfield players who would grease up their vests so that players couldn't hold onto them. One of those players, in the back row, second from left, is Frank Massing, a pattern maker at EMI, who enjoyed playing guitar and banjo. *(Submitted by Kenneth Massing, grandson of Frank Massing).*

Cut above the rest

Shown in this turn-of-the-century photo is John Sebastian in his meat market which was located at 412 W. 18th St. John (on the far right with the moustache) lived on the second floor above the market with his wife Emma. *(Submitted by Evelyn Shelhamer, great-niece of John Sebastian).*

Historic Eagle

This is an early photo of the Eagle Hotel in Waterford. It was built in 1826 by Thomas King and quickly became the center of social and civic activities. The ballroom on the third floor has a spring floor. The hotel housed many important guests including Zachary Taylor. It was a major stage coach stop and later a bus stop. By the 1860s, Waterford had become a resort and the Eagle was advertised as one of the finest accommodations in the country. In addition, it has national significance as being adjacent to the Old Fort LeBoeuf – the fort in Waterford first occupied by the French, then the British and finally, the Americans. *(Submitted by the Fort LeBoeuf Historical Society).*

Waterford Depot

The Waterford Station, commonly called "The Depot," was erected in the mid 1850s at the time the Philadelphia-Erie railroad was being built. It was located one mile east of the Waterford Borough because the town residents did not want the railroad running through the town. There was a telegraph office located in the building and other buildings quickly sprang up including a hotel/grocery store, cider mill, Sulky Rake Factory, ice house, a school and a Catholic church. *(Submitted by the Fort LeBoeuf Historical Society).*

Home sweet home

This 1905 photo depicts the Eller family in front of their home at 2669 Myrtle St. The home is still standing today, but has been re-numbered 2671. Note the amount of land around the home. Today, there are houses on both sides of the home. The people in the photo are: Clara, Anna, Lizzetta, Peter and George Eller. *(Submitted by Diane Johns, Anna's granddaughter).*

1800s Wedding Portrait

Harriet "Hattie" and Fred Harmon were married in May of 1872 when this photo is assumed to have been taken. Hattie is the great-granddaughter of Nicholas Stough, one of the five founding members of the St. John's Lutheran Church in Erie, who settled in Erie after receiving a land grant from the government for serving in the Revolutionary War. It is unknown how much land he was actually given, but he came to own 168 acres in the area of the Millcreek Mall. Fred Harmon drove horses for barges on the old Meadville Canal and was then employed at the Erie Car Works and Lake Shore Railroad before starting his own greenhouse in 1872 at 2208 Liberty St. *(Submitted by Diane Harriet Boesch, great-niece of Hattie Stough Harmon).*

The school year autograph book was alive and well in the 1870s. Here, George Burton tells all about himself, including his interest in medicine. His family is well-known in the Erie funeral industry even today. *(Submitted by John Baker).*

Mr. Geo. H. Burton Erie Penna. Sept. 1877

Your Favorite
1. Color? Cardinal (chair)
2. Flower? Heliotrope—Rose—
3. Tree? The noble oak—
4. Object in Nature? Horse—Handsome woman
5. Hour in the Day? 12 o'clock—and 9 eve.
6. Season of the Year? Spring—
7. Perfume? Geranium—
8. Gem? Moss agate—Amethyst
9. Style of Beauty? Strawberry-blonde
10. Names, Male and Female? Frank Chas, Clara—
11. Painters? Education neglected—Earle Graylock—
12. Musicians? No opinion—
13. Piece of Sculpture? Forced Prayer—
14. Poets? I pass!
15. Poetesses? ditto—
16. Prose Authors? Sir Walter Scott—Miss Alcott
17. Character in Romance? St. Elmo—
18. _____ in History? "Chris"—
19. Book to take up for an hour? Day Book—
20. What Book (not religious) would you part with last? Bank Book—

21. What epoch would you choose to have lived in? B. C.
22. Where would you like to live? With You
23. What is your favorite amusement? Nothing
24. What is your favorite occupation? Study of Medicine
25. What trait of character do you most admire in man? Firmness and courage.
26. What trait of character do you most admire in woman? Truthfulness
27. What trait of character do you most detest in each? Deceitfulness & Selfishness
28. If not yourself, who would you rather be? Some one else
29. What is your idea of happiness? A home, and a brown eyed wife
30. What is your idea of misery? Loss of fortune, and respect of friends
31. What is your bête noir? Entertain, a girl I detest
32. "   " dream? I never dream
33. What is your favorite game? Base Ball
34. What do you believe to be your distinguishing characteristics? Not developed yet
35. If married, what do you believe to be the distinguishing characteristics of your better-half?
36. What is the sublimest passion of which human nature is capable? Love, and Hate
37. What are the sweetest words in the world?
38. What are the saddest words? Don't you know I don't approve of th
39. What is your aim in life? Eminence, Happiness, and Truth
40. What is your motto?

8

B.F. Fields Moving Co.

This 1908 photo depicts a young Ben Fields when he began his moving company business at the turn of the century. The firm is still in operation as the B.F. Fields Moving and Storage company located at 945 Downing Ave. in Erie. *(Submitted by Erwin Marz, stepgrandson of Ben Fields).*

Super cooper

Frank and Elizabeth (Tretter) Ohmer are shown in their formal wedding portrait taken in the late 1800s. Frank worked as a "cooper" – a person who made wooden barrels – in Buffalo and would travel home to Erie on the weekends. Frank and Elizabeth lived in east Erie, had nine children and also raised their granddaughter, Bette. *(Submitted by Bette Williams, granddaughter).*

Clapper buildings had something for everyone

The Clapper family and their grocery and dry goods store are shown in this late 1800s era photo. The family home and store were located at 8978 Main St. in McKean, Pa. The house on the right was the home of Peleg and Emma Hauck Clapper who, in 1888, had a building constructed adjacent to their home that became a general store and dry goods shop. The two buildings were connected with a doorway between them. The store portion of the building did not have a second floor, but instead had a balcony where shoes were sold that ran the length of the building. At the back of the building, a stairway gave entrance to the top floors which contained a basketball court where local men and boys would gather to play (as there were no high schools in the area at the time). According to the photo contributor, the markings on the floor are still visible today (although they are under carpet). The basketball court area was also rented for local dances – usually square dances. In 1929, Peleg's son, Dr. Guy Clapper, bought the store building and remodeled it into a home for his family and office space for his practice. To this day, the building remains a residence occupied by a Clapper family member on Route 99 (formerly Main Street) in McKean. *(Submitted by Jeanne Clapper O'Brien, granddaughter of Peleg and Emma).*

Early Erie carpeters

This c. 1890s photo shows Gustave Baumann, August Baumann, Joseph Baumann and their horse, Maude, in front of their business – Baumann & Son Carpet Cleaning Works. The horse and buggy were used to deliver carpet (in the winter, they used a horse and sleigh). Carpet Cleaning Works was the predecessor to Baumann Bros. Carpetowne which is still in operation today on East 12th Street in downtown Erie and run by fourth generation family member, Bruce Baumann. Gustave Baumann, who fought in the Civil War, started the Baumann Bros. business in 1885 after coming to Erie from Germany where he was a carpet installer and upholsterer. *(Submitted by Bruce Baumann).*

Strapping young men

Peter Felbinger and his son, John, pose for this early 1900s photo in Peter's harness shop on Peach Street (where Krug's parking lot is now). The Felbinger family lived on the second floor of the shop. *(Submitted by Evelyn Shelhamer, great granddaughter of Peter).*

All in the family

This multi-generation family portrait was taken in 1906 in Wattsburg and depicts the Duryee/Whipple/Truax Families. The family members shown are (first row, l-r), Clinton Whipple; Clinton's grandmother, Sarah Duryee; Baby Clair Whipple (on Sarah's lap); Walter Whipple, brother to Clinton and Clair; Ernest Duryee, grandfather to children; Leon Whipple, brother to Clinton, Clair and Walter. In the second row, (l-r) are Frank Duryee, Clinton's Uncle; Will Duryee, Clinton's Uncle; Jeannie Duryee Whipple, mother of small children; Mr. Truax, brother-in-law to Jennie; Nellie Duryee Truax, sister to Jennie. *(Submitted by Marjorie Whipple, daughter of Clinton Whipple).*

School days

Students of the Harrison School – a one room schoolhouse (8 grades) located the southwest area of McKean Township – pose for this c. 1898 photo. Two of the students in this photo are identified. On the far right is Harry E. Steadman and to his right is his brother, Ray J. Steadman. *(Submitted by Marian Russell, Ray's daughter).*

From hogs to hams

Spring was the time for butchering as evidenced by this 1906 hog butchering scene taking place in the backyard of the Will Kratzke home on North Creek Road in Girard. The men in the photo are (l-r), Will Kratzke, Carl Wright (a neighbor), and A. John Angerer (sharpening knife). In the background of the left side of the photo, you can make out the Nickel Plate railroad trestle. *(Submitted by Fritz Angerer, son of A. John Angerer, grandson of Will Kratzke).*

11

The Turn of the Century
1900-1909

Air flight, automobiles, boy scouts and the beginnings of global communication were all introduced in the first decade of the 20th century. Erie gets its first automobile, swimming pool, trolley service to Buffalo and a visit from President McKinley.

● The City of Erie imposes a 10-mph speed limit for all "horseless carriages" in town.

● Erie Bishop Tobias Mullen's death in 1900 leaves Erie mourning the loss of one of its most enduring religious figures. During his 30 year tenure with the Erie Diocese, he oversaw the construction of St. Peter Cathedral, organized a Catholic cemetery for all of the city's parishes, handled the organization of Saint Vincent Hospital, built an orphanage and organized the area's first retirement home.

● The Erie Electric Motor Co. begins developing Hopkin's Grove into Waldameer Park in 1900. The trolley company adds a bathhouse and carousel to the park in an effort to increase electrical trolley business by luring city residents to the lake front.

● A four story annex to Saint Vincent's Hospital opens (1900).

● The Erie County Library enjoys its first full year in a new building, located at South Park Row and French Street (1900).

● On Sept. 4, 1901, President McKinley is greeted by 10,000 Erie residents as he passes through Erie on his way to Buffalo to attend the Pan-American Exposition where he was shot on Sept. 6.

● In 1901, the Roth brothers begin to convert their business from bicycles to automobiles. More than 100 years later, Roth Cadillac remains the oldest Cadillac dealership in the country.

● Jackson Koehler, founder of Erie Brewing Co. and the first man to own an automobile in Erie, died in 1903 at the age of 52.

● Erie's first pool is built inside the YMCA (1904).

● On July 2, 1906, an elaborate celebration marks the opening of St. Patrick's Church.

● Local aviator, Fred Owens, made the first recorded flight over Erie on Aug. 7, 1909 – not in an airplane, but in an airship. The balloon floated over the city during its trip from Four Mile Creek park to City Hall and back again, a trip of about 30 minutes.

● General Electric starts work on a $1 million building project on East Lake Road in 1908.

● Trolley service between Buffalo and Erie begins in 1909.

● The average man's weekly salary in 1909 is $25 and will go toward household items such as shoes, which cost about $2 a pair, curtains, 39 cents each, a rocking chair, $19, or coffee, 25 cents a pound. A two-story house with ten rooms was about $4,000 and a new coat cost $5.

No peach jam

This photo, taken at the southwest corner of 22nd and Peach streets in the early 1900s, shows A.F. Schultz Co., wholesale tobacconists. The sign behind the utility pole on the corner advertises Piedmont cigarettes, ten for nine cents and twenty for fifteen cents. Next door, to the left, is the Home Bakery and above that is the Majestic Tea Co. (in those days every neighborhood had a bakery and a tea store). Tea stores were the forerunner of the chain supermarkets, but generally dealt in nothing but tea, coffee and spices. To the far left is St. John's Lutheran Church which was built in 1861. *(Submitted by St. John's Lutheran Church).*

Team Mohawk

The northwest portion of Erie's Fourth Ward was once known as "Jerusalem" by the residents who lived there and was considered by many to be the "cradle of Erie baseball." The Mohawks, one of the teams from this area, pose for this c. 1911 photo. Two men are identified – Paul Kapsar (kneeling in the center of the photo) and Paul's brother, John Kapsar, in the top row, far left. *(Submitted by Robert Kapsar, son of Paul Kapsar).*

Bell pulls

"Kentucky Bell" is prepared to pull his owners, Robert and Annie Tuttle, in this 1900s era Harborcreek photo. (*Donated to the Harborcreek Historical Society by Robert W. Tuttle).*

Get some lunch, shoot some pool

This photo, taken at the corner of Walnut and 15th streets (where the Nuova Aurora Club now stands), shows one of Erie's first Italian settlers, Gaetano Spadacene, who poses in front of his Spadacene Co. Cafe. Next door is the pool room operated by Gaetano's nephew, Frank Sena. Spadacene's family was from Tuscany, Italy. *(Submitted by Cecilia Carmisino Ross, niece of Frank Sena, great-niece of Gaetano Spadacene).*

Hospitable hospital

Hamot Hospital (as it was first named) began as a five-room, three-ward hospital when the family of French adventurer, Pierre S.V. Hamot, donated the family homestead for that purpose. The building was donated on the conditions that the hospital always be called "Hamot" and that no one would ever be refused admittance to the hospital on the basis of "sect, sex or condition of life." When Hamot Hospital opened its doors on July 1, 1881, it had the capacity to house 25 patients. *(Submitted by Karen Clement).*

Hospital History

Saint Vincent Hospital (as it was first named) opened on September 5, 1875. The original building cost $7,000 and consisted of three stories with a furnished basement containing the operating room. *(Submitted by Karen Clement).*

Fuller's first
Shown here in this 1912 photo is the first firetruck owned by the Fuller Hose Company in North East. Fire chief, Carl Diehl, is driving the truck. (Submitted by Lewis Diehl, son of Carl).

Baby's baptism
Thelma Kathryn Altstadt, daughter of Ellen and Francis Altstadt, is shown in her baptism dress in this 1904 photo. Thelma grew up, married Norman Gleason and they had three daughters – Norma, Jane and Betty. Thelma's beautiful baptism gown was worn by her great granddaughter, Caroline Granahan, when she was baptized in 1982 – nearly 80 years later. *(Submitted by Mary Ann Granahan, Thelma's granddaughter and Caroline's mother).*

Wattsburg-Pa — from Erie Hill

Wattsburg before the fires and floods

This 1907 postcard depicts what Wattsburg looked like before fires and floods took their toll on the borough in the 20th century. A fire along main street in 1928 ravaged an entire block, destroying most of the business district, including the landmark Wattsburg Hotel which was built in 1882. It was said that the firefighters drained French Creek in their efforts to put out the blaze. Two terrible floods also occurred, one in 1939 and the other in 1947, damaging individual residences. There has been no more flooding of this magnitude since the completion of the French Creek Reservoir and Dam project in the 1960s. *(Submitted by T.G. Rouse).*

Sittin' on the dock of the bay

Arthur Roth kicks back at his bachelor pad – a houseboat on Lake Erie – in this c. 1910 photo. *(Submitted by Evelyn Shelhamer, Arthur's granddaughter).*

Keystone cops

Erie City Police Officers pose in this c. 1906 photo taken in front of Old City Hall which was located on Peach Street between South Park Row and Seventh streets. According to the photo contributor, the photo looks to have been taken from the Seventh Street side as you can see the basement stairs (leading to the jail) on either side of the staircase the officers are standing on. The only man identified in this photo is John Fletcher in the front row, sixth from the left, next to the dog. Notice that the officers all carried batons instead of guns. *(Submitted by Robert Kapsar, great grandson of John Fletcher).*

Let there be light

Harley D. Carpenter (man on the left in this photo) founded Harley D. Carpenter & Sons and Carpenter Electric Supplies & Contracting in 1906, opening his first electric shop in Meadville, Pa. Harley was known for developing electric utilities in rural areas long before large companies were interested in the service. He began the electric service in Conneaut Lake, Pa. in 1912 and expanded into Cochranton, Saegertown, Spartansburg and Sparta. By 1952, Carpenter Light, Heat & Power had 9,000 customers in 10 rural townships in Crawford County and 500 miles of rural lines. In 1960, the company was sold to Penelec/PennPower. Harley's son, Paul Carpenter, managed the electrical supply store for 59 years and expanded the Erie location to include 1517 and 1519 State St. In 1995, Paul turned the business over to his son and current owner, Gary Carpenter, who had worked in the family business since 1972. Gary further expanded the business by adding 1515 and 1511 State St. The business is still in operation today, serving the electrical and lighting needs of the Erie area. *(Submitted by Gary Carpenter).*

Go speed racer, go!

Russell Randall Leo tries out some sort of homemade riding toy in this 1907 photo taken at his family's home at 232 W. 2nd St. As an adult, Russel worked at General Electric and married Alberta Glendine. They had two children – Sarah and Jean. *(Photo submitted by Jean Leo Moore, daughter).*

Old-fashioned water park

Donald Sexauer plays in front of his family's boathouse on Lake Erie. The boathouse was built by Donald's father, Grover Cleveland Sexauer, who was a carpenter by trade and lived at the boathouse with his wife, Mae, and son, Donald. They later had a second son, Richard. *(Submitted by Patricia Surrena, daughter of Donald).*

Pump engine parade

The Erie Fire Department's pump engine is shown participating in a parade on South Park Row in this 1900s photo. The man on the back of the pumper is Erie firefighter George Warren Banister (the driver is unidentified). (*Submitted by Stella Auer, George's granddaughter*).

Round and round it goes

This 1914 postcard depicts the Merry-go-round at Waldamere Park (note the different spelling of the park name then). (*Submitted by Jane Kressel*).

Merry-go-round in Waldemere Park, Erie, Pa.

Timber!

The photo at left illustrates the size of virgin timber that was instrumental in Union Mills (later known as Union City) becoming the "Chair Center of the World." Standing to the right of the logs are Alfred Caflisch and Hank Cottrell. Alfred's father owned the factory pictured here, the Union City Chair Company, which was located on Market Street. The trees pictured here are actually small compared to the ones found 100 years before. *(Submitted by Union City Historical Society Officers).*

Prominent Harborcreek home

Mrs. C. Guy Wakeley holds her infant daughter, Jeanette, 6 mos., on the steps of a prominent Harborcreek home that is still in existence at 2701 Nagle Rd. between Rolling Ridge Parkway and Briarwood Drive. When this photo was taken, in 1924, the house was part of the Henry Farm and the Nagle Road was called Henry Road. Jeanette went on to attend Brookside School, Harborcreek Central and graduated from the new Harbor Creek High School in 1942. *(Submitted by Jeanette Koskie).*

The Teen Years
1910-1919

*W*orld War I, the first telephone call, the raising of the Niagara and the great Mill Creek flood were all part of the second decade of the 20th century in the Erie area. President William Taft visits Erie, the first local theater is opened and Erie's first licensed pilot flies across Lake Erie.

● By the end of 1910, eight automobile dealerships serve Erie, a reflection of the growing popularity of cars.

● Thomas Edison unveils his latest invention, talking motion pictures, in West Orange, N.J. in 1910.

● President William Taft visits Erie for an overnight stay on Sept. 18, 1911. Taft is the guest of Charles Strong and his family and is guarded by more than 60 police officers. He is in town to attend the annual Erie Chamber of Commerce banquet.

● More than 1,500 people perish in the frigid Atlantic Ocean as the great Titanic sank on April 15, 1912, two hours and 40 minutes after striking an iceberg.

● After nearly 90 years in its watery grave, the Brig Niagara is raised from the mud of Misery Bay in early March of 1913 and refurbished for the 100th anniversary celebration of the victory of Oliver Hazard Perry at the Battle of Lake Erie during the War of 1812.

● Erie's first licensed pilot, Earl Sandt, records the first flight across Lake Erie (1912).

● In 1913, The Erie Symphonic Orchestra is organized under Erie native, Frank Kohler. While the 52-piece orchestra is disbanded during the war, it is revived as the philharmonic under the tutelage of Henry Bethuel Vincent, who organizes the Little Playhouse in 1916.

● Erie's first mechanized firefighting equipment is purchased in 1915. However, the last horse-drawn equipment is not retired until 1922.

● The first public transcontinental telephone conversation takes place between Alexander Graham Bell in New York and his assistant Thomas Watson in San Francisco, Ca. on Jan. 25, 1915.

● Swollen by 6 inches of rain that pounded the area for 13 hours, Mill Creek breached its banks on Aug. 4, 1915. The water was held back by a blocked culvert that ran beneath 26th Street and formed a lake that some historians estimate grew to be 30 feet deep before the culvert gave way, unleashing a wall of water nearly 14 feet high. The death count is unclear, with the numbers ranging from 25-37 dead. At least $2 million in property damage was caused.

● Henry Vincent opens the Little Playhouse in 1916, one of Erie's first local theaters.

● The United States enters World War I in Europe in 1917 and begins to consolidate its standings as a world power.

● George Ryder, 19, is the first Erie resident killed in World War I in 1917.

● The Right Reverend John Mark Gannon is named auxiliary bishop of the Erie Diocese in 1918.

● The 19th Amendment, giving women the right to vote, is approved by Congress and submitted to the states for ratification (1919).

● All of Erie welcomes home Company G after World War I ends in 1919. Thousands line the streets to honor Erie's soldiers.

● Work begins on the new Academy High School (1919).

● The foundation of Lord Corp. is laid when Henry Lord starts experimenting with rubber-bonded-to-metal components for noise and vibration control in 1919.

Pontiac proprietor

Longnecker Pontiac, located at 126 E. 12th St., was owned by Carl Peter Longnecker (in the gray suit) in the photo at left taken in the space behind the formal offices at Longnecker Pontiac c. 1915. Above is a photo of auto mechanics c. 1915 in the repair shop. An exterior view of the dealership in 1938 is shown in the photo at right. *(Submitted by Carole Longnecker Groters, great niece of Carl Longnecker).*

24

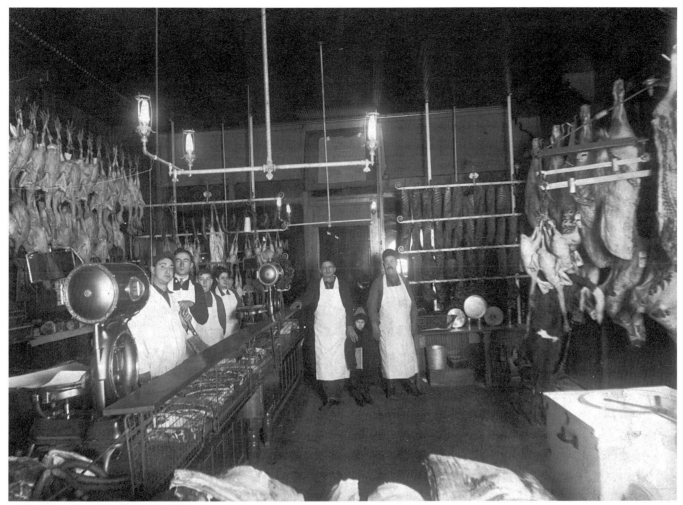

All the meat that's fit to eat

Smith's Butcher Shop was located in the 800 block of Parade Street when this 1910 photo was taken. The woman at the end of the counter is Carrie Smith Mackrell, all others are unidentified. Notice the gas lights, old scales and the different cuts of meat hanging on the walls. (*Submitted by Mary Theiss, Carrie's granddaughter*).

No longer in Misery

Pictured here is the original hull of the Niagara that was removed from Misery Bay in 1913 and restored for the 100th anniversary celebration of Perry's victory at the Battle of Lake Erie. *(Photo courtesy of Erie Maritime Museum).*

Workers get a raise

Men who are working to raise the Niagara from Misery Bay pose for this 1913 photo. *(From the Erie Times-News archives).*

The Resurrection of the Niagara

By
Joseph Reilly

A stately ship, she rides once more
The sun-kissed water of the bay;
And once again, she hears the roar,
Of many guns at break-of-day.

She feels the thrill from stem to stern,
And wakens from her century's sleep,
Full-rigged with masts and snowy sails,
A sea bird rose from the deep.

And once again, at set of sun,
She slowly sails, across the bar,
And blending with the farewell gun,
The church bells echo from afar.

Poetic beauty

Joseph Reilly, shown here in this 1910s photo with his niece, Thelma Kathryn Altstadt, at Presque Isle State Park, was a poet and an artist. One of Joseph's Poems – "The Resurrection of the Niagara" (at left) was written in honor of the Niagara's 1913 restoration. *(Submitted by Mary Ann Granahan, Thelma's granddaughter, Joseph's great-great niece).*

11th & Millcreek, Aug. 3rd, 1915, Erie, Pa.

Where Quinn & Newmer Buildings were destroyed by flood, Aug, 3rd, 1915, Erie, Pa.

The mighty Mill Creek flood

The flooding of Mill Creek on Aug. 3, 1915 was one of the most devastating natural disasters to hit the Erie area, resulting in an estimated death toll of 25 to 37 individuals. The flood occurred after 5.77 inches of rain fell on the area. *(Submitted by Paul Gaeckle).*

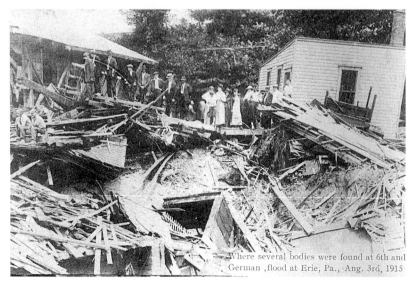

Where several bodies were found at 6th and German ,flood at Erie, Pa., Ang. 3rd, 1915

Families made homeless between Eleventh and Twelfth on Mill Creek, Erie, Pa. Aug. 3rd, 1915

Family fruit

Siblings, (l-r) Josephine Sunseri Picardo, Paul Sunseri and Vincy Sunseri Cipolla work the family's fruit stand inside the Twelfth Street Market in Erie in 1929. Their father, Frank Sunseri, started the business around 1911 and had both a retail stand and a wholesale business. Josephine's son, Mike Picardo, carried on the family tradition and currently operates Picardo Farms in west Erie County. *(Submitted by Phyllis Hlavin, daughter of Vincy Sunseri Cipolla).*

Pipe parade

This Tellers-Sommerhof Organ, as seen in the Perry Centennial parade in 1913, was probably the first pipe organ to join a parade. Two men hand pumped wind supply for the organ while a third played music along the way. Waving the flag is Herman J. Tellers, former president of the Tellers Organ Co., Inc. and father of present owner and president, Henry C. Tellers. The other boy is Roy Sommerhof, son of the late W.A. Sommerhof. *(Submitted by Elizabeth Tellers Schaaf, daughter of Herman Tellers, for Gust Olson, the first employee of Tellers Organ Company).*

48-star flag wavers

Teacher, Edith Heidler, poses with her students for this 1918-1919 class photo. Edith taught grades 1-8 at both Hershey and Swanville Elementary schools. Note the flag only had 48 stars as the last two U.S. states had not yet been admitted. Edith married Jack Osterberg and they had three children. *(Submitted by Evelyn Osterberg, daughter).*

Rat tale

Did you ever wonder how the ladies at the turn of the century got the puffy look to their hair as seen in this 1912 photo? According to Harriet Duddenhoeffer Boesch, pictured here with her husband, Frank Boesch (both seated) and her sister, Lillian Dudenhoeffer Kane (standing), they got the look, not by teasing but by adding wads of hair that had fallen out. "All the ladies kept jars on their dressers for the hairs that would come out as they combed their hair. This hair was kept in a wad and called a 'rat.' When their hair was being done, the ladies would comb their real hair forward, pin in the rat and then carefully comb the real hair over the rat to create the puffy look seen in the pictures." *(Submitted by Diane Harriet Boesch, granddaughter of Harriet Dudenhoeffer Boesch).*

Oldest Lutheran church stands tall

St. John's Lutheran Church, the oldest Lutheran Church in Erie, was constructed in 1861 (records show that the basement was built in 1861, but it's unclear when the building was actually finished) on land deeded to the church from the Braun family. The church, located on 23rd and Peach streets (then known as "Federal Way") used to be served by pastors from the Meadville area who would arrive by horse and carriage until the church got their own pastor, Adolph Benze, around 1890. *(Submitted by St. John's Lutheran Church).*

Pocketful of posies

Irwin Fredrick Gaeckle poses with some flowers and a play doll in this 1914 photo taken at his home on Fourth and Poplar streets in Erie. Irwin grew up to become a pressman at the Erie Daily Times and had two sons – Paul and Fred. *(Submitted by Paul Gaeckle).*

International bartending team

The caption on the back of this photo reads "The Irish and Dutch Team" – referring to the two bartenders shown in the photo, an Irishman, Eddie Sherry, and a Dutchman, George Stephany, working at the "Arcade" in Erie in this 1910 photo. (*Submitted by Mary Theiss, George's granddaughter*).

Ready and waiting

A group of Erie firefighters pose with their firefighting gear for this 1915 photo taken behind the #7 fire station at West 26th and Peach streets. *(Courtesy of the Firefighters Historical Museum, Inc.).*

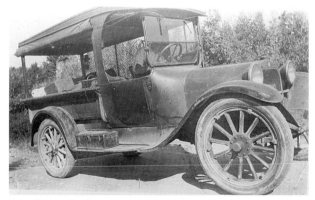

Dodge delivers

This 1919 photo depicts the Dodge truck that George Auer (in driver's seat) used to deliver sheet metal for Auer Sheet Metal – a business that he owned with his brother, Leo in the late 1910s. *(Submitted by Richard Auer, George's son).*

Volland family portrait

The Volland family, pictured in this July 4, 1911 photo, has a rich Erie history. They are all descendants of Charles Volland, a native of Germany who came to Erie in 1854. He learned the printers trade and worked in Erie newspaper offices until 1860. He later went on to establish his own grocery business at the corner of Eighth and Ash streets. According to his great-granddaughter, Mr. Volland was a founding father of the Erie Maennerchor Club. Pictured (first row, l-r) are Bernard Volland, Richard Kennedy, Clifford Ives, Ethel Ives, Marion Volland, Evelyn Volland; 2nd row, Charles Kennedy, Blanche Volland, Frances Albrecht, Thelma (Sally) Volland; 3rd row, Minnie Volland Kennedy, Mamie Volland Schaal, Mamie Volland, August Volland, Emma Volland, Henry Volland, Louise Volland Albrecht, Elizabeth "Lizzie" Volland Ives; 4th row, August Albrecht, Clarence Schaal Albrecht (holding Wallace), Otto Volland, Charles Volland, George Kennedy, Fred Volland and Silas Ives. *(Submitted by Kathleen Kennedy, daughter of Richard Kennedy).*

Girard's first delivery truck

Pictured here are J.P. (Jim) Sherman and his helpers Fritz Angerer and Lena (Susie) Ellwanger in the first truck ever used for deliveries in the Girard area. The truck was a 1910 International Harvester Co. truck and the photo was taken in front of Mr. Sherman's Hardware store in Girard in 1946. Mr. Sherman was known for many other "firsts" in Girard, including the first gasoline pump, first curbside pump, first to sell pneumatic tires in town, first barrel of automotive oil, first flashing sign and the first fluorescent lighting in a Girard store. Fritz Angerer and Cliff Miller bought the hardware store from Mr. Sherman in 1951 and operated it until 1979. *(Submitted by Fritz Angerer).*

Early beach boys (and girls)

According to the contributor, this snapshot was taken at Waldameer Park in 1916. Notice the row of bathhouses and the cumbersome "swimming suits" worn by the boys and girls in the background. Pictured (l-r beginning with the girl in the white dress and bonnet) are: Florence Stritzinger, Nellie Stritzinger, Mary Stritzinger, John Mann and Florence Weber. *(Submitted by Lois Baker, daughter of Florence Stritzinger).*

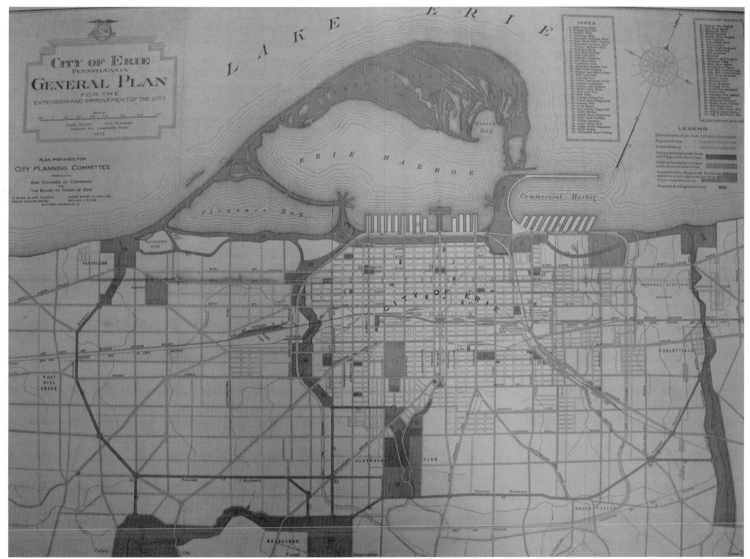

Planning for the future

This "general plan" for the extension and improvement of the City of Erie is dated 1913. Note the two bays and trails planned for Presque Isle. It's also interesting to note that this plan called for a park to encircle the city. Frontier Park is the only remnant of this plan today.

The Roarin' Twenties
1920-1929

*P*rohibition, the Great Depression, motorized buses and the founding of Erie Insurance Exchange and two local colleges were all part of the 1920s in Erie, Pa.

● Prohibition arrived in the U.S. on Jan. 16, 1920 with the passage of the Volstead Act. Alcoholic beverages could no longer be produced, transported, sold or consumed in public. This act lead to the Erie Mayor's announcement on Sept. 8, 1920 that any police officer accepting a drink while on duty will be fined five days pay after allegations that officers were being influenced when they should have been enforcing the Volstead Act.

● Academy High School opened its doors on Sept. 7, 1920 with John C. Diehl as principal.

● Eight are killed, 18 injured on Oct. 20, 1920 when a Buffalo passenger train is sideswiped by another train between Sassafras and Myrtle streets. An incorrect switch was pulled, allowing both trains access to the tracks.

● Work begins on East High School (1921).

● On Nov. 26, 1921, the Mill Creek tube was completed and the city is protected from another disastrous flood such as the one in 1915.

● A gasoline explosion fuels a fire that destroys the Keystone Fish Co. plant on Erie's bayfront (1923).

● Presque Isle becomes a state park (1922).

● The Booker T. Washington Center is founded (1923).

● A fire at Stanley Brothers Furniture Co., 12th and Parade streets on Sept. 24, 1923, destroys $100,000 worth of property including numerous buildings, a fire truck and three cars. Several firefighters were injured, including the Fire Chief.

● St. Joseph's Orphanage was dedicated on July 20, 1924.

● Mumps are the leading health threat facing Erie residents, along with chicken pox, scarlet fever, typhoid fever, whooping cough and tuberculosis (1925).

● Villa Maria College opens as an all-women's school (1925).

● Erie Insurance Exchange opens its doors under the leadership of H.O. Hirt and O.G. Crawford after the two meet while working on another business. The exchange opens in the Scott building where the Avalon Hotel is now located. The company adopts the motto, "the ERIE is above all in service" and follows up by opening its door 24 hours a day, seven days a week.

● Motorized buses appear on city streets for the first time on Dec. 5, 1925.

● Classes begin at Mercyhurst College in 1926 despite a strike that halted all work at the construction site leading the Sisters of Mercy to take matters into their own hands and complete the project themselves.

● Erie's first radio station – WRAK – starts its broadcasts in 1927. The radio station of Times Publishing is quickly joined on air by a Dispatch station (their rival newspaper).

● The Twelfth Street Market opens its doors; the two-story building offers a variety of fresh food (1927).

● Fourteen stores and three homes are destroyed in a Wattsburg blaze that threatens the entire city. All but three businesses in the district are lost. Damage is estimated at $100,000 (Sept. 14, 1928).

● Stock market reports turn grim on Oct. 29, 1929. After a series of dips and swells, it begins to dive. The worst will hit Erie in the early 1930s.

Working on the railroad

This group of men were all workers at the New York Central railroad car shops in Erie, Pa. in the 1920s.
(Submitted by John Szympruch).

I'm in the mood for a melody

The Melody Sweethearts played in various venues in the late 1920s. Members of the band and the instruments they played were: Hilda Hawley, trumpet; Helen Christoph, saxophone; Dorothy Little, saxophone; Margaret Arbuckle, violin; Mildred Miles, piano; Laura Fitting, banjo; Carrie Spacek, drums; Marge Herpick, saxophone. Laura Fitting went on to marry Earl Hossman in 1934. According to Earl, they ran off and got married in Ripley by George Bennet, Justice of the Peace, for $10. *(Submitted by Earl Hossman).*

Gravity aided gas tank

Shown at right is the gas pump in front of Kane's Korner Grocery Store on West 26th Street in Erie in the 1920s. The gas pump was operated by rotating the handle until the desired amount of gas came up in the container at the top of the pump. Then, relying on gravity, the gas drained into the gas tank. *(Submitted by Diane Harriet Boesch).*

Ready to serve

Employees of the Kresge Company (department store) at 904 State St. pose for this 1920s era photo. Notice the prices on the merchandise on display. Employees listed on the back of the photo are: Gertrude Schaaf, May Pennock, Isabelle Ragen, Margaret Lubel, Bernice Holden, Nina Wickurie, Pearl Keller, Daisy Forry, Clara Fromknecht, Flo Stritzinger (Contributor's mother), Gertrude Matters, Hazel Parsons, Mrs. Lattimore, Kathryn Young, A.C. Cummins, Marie Kohler, Helen Malinowski, Lucy DiNunzio, Julia Olson, Louise Marnella, Marie Delaney, Chas. Shaffer, Anna Breter, Gertrude Hamm and John Willett. *(Contributed by Lois Baker).*

Early swimsuit models

Florence Stritzinger (far left) models the newest 1920s swimwear with her friends. Notice the swim caps that were very popular in the '20s. *(Submitted by Lois Baker, daughter of Florence Stritzinger).*

Basketball boys

This basketball team was part of the Erie YMCA basketball league in the early 1920s. Pictured are: first row (l-r) Emerson Johnson, Leonard Grumblett, Robert Serr; second row (l-r) Luke Crawford, unidentified, Russell R. Leo. *(Submitted by Jean Leo Moore).*

Lifesavers at your service

A group of U.S. Lifesaving Service officers sail on Lake Erie in this 1920s photo. The U.S. Lifesaving Service later became the U.S. Coast Guard. *(Submitted by Patricia Surrena whose great-uncle Bill Sexauer was a Lifesaver).*

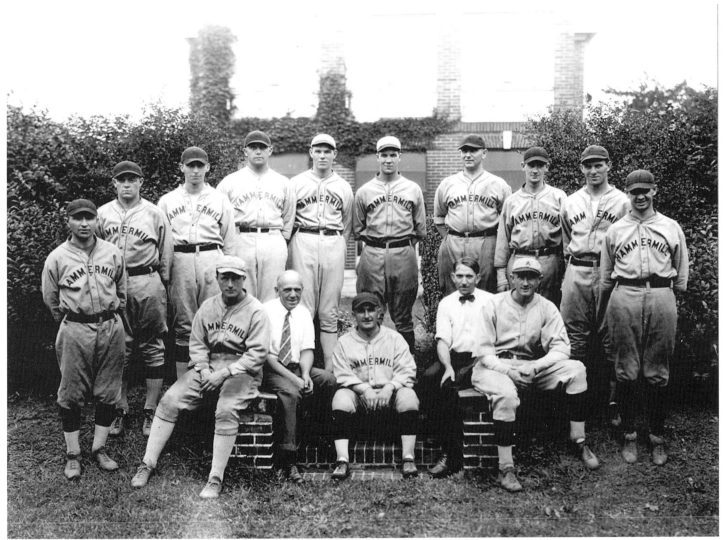

We are the champions, we are the champions...

Pictured here are the members of the Hammermill baseball team who won the Industrial and City Championship in 1929. The first man in the front row on the left side is Charles "Bus" Downing who served on Erie City Council for many years. During his tenure, the Downing Golf Course in Harborcreek was built and named after him. *(Submitted by Ann and Charlie Downing, children of Bus Downing).*

Porch pals

Young Sam, 6, and Jim, 4, Baldi pose on the porch of their parents home on Plum Street in this 1928 photo. *(Submitted by Linda Evans, niece of Sam and Jim).*

What's red and black and full of melodies?

Pictured in this 1926 photo are Claron Farr and his Red & Black Melody Boys along with all of their instruments. Carl J. Peterson, second from the left, went on to teach music at Academy High School and later became the Coordinator of Music for all of the Erie City Schools. *(Submitted by Sheldon Peterson, son of Carl Peterson).*

Swan dive

A swimmer takes a swan dive into the Downtown YMCA's pool in this c. 1920s photo. YMCAs across the country have built a national reputation on quality swimming education. Today, the YMCA of Greater Erie operates 11 pools and each year gives nearly 9,000 swim lessons. In fact, the YMCA was responsible for building the very first public swimming pool in Erie in 1904. *(Submitted by the YMCA of Greater Erie).*

Motorcycle men

Erie City Motorcycle Police Officers pose in this c. 1920s photo taken in front of Old City Hall which was located on Peach Street between Sixth and Seventh streets. Old City Hall was built in 1884 and was considered by many to be a great piece of architecture. The city jail was located in the basement of the building. *(Submitted by Midas Muffler, 410 W. 12th St.).*

Lighthouse ladies

Mae Sexauer, Edith Sexauer and Mame Bray pose in front of the Erie Harbor North Pierhead Light in this 1920s photo. The lighthouse was originally constructed in 1830 as a wooden pierhead beacon. The original tower was later destroyed by a passing vessel in 1857. The light was rebuilt in 1858 with stronger materials, and still stands today. The 34 foot tall beacon was constructed of wrought iron, and encased in steel plates. The black and white banded tower has successfully weathered the powerful winter storms through many decades. The tower was moved 190 feet in 1882, and again 509 feet in 1940 when the beacon was automated. A solar powered modern lens replaced the original fourth order Fresnel lens in 1995, and is still an active beacon. The original lens was then transferred to the new Erie Maritime Museum across the bay. The original keeper's quarters is located within the nearby lifesaving station, but the original fog signal horn and bell have since been removed. *(Photo submitted by Patricia Surrena, granddaughter of Mae Sexauer. Historical information provided by Rod Watson at rodwatson.com).*

Hammermill helpers

Workers are captured in action in this photo taken at the Hammermill Paper Co. in the 1920s. At far left, Albert Sieber, a blacksmith by trade who immigrated with his wife, Louise Baier Sieber, from Germany in the 1900s. They had eleven children: Bertha, Olga, Clara, Louise, Albert, Carl, Herman, Fred, Don, Edward and Paul. *(Submitted by Kathleen Amann Derda, granddaughter of Albert Sieber).*

Waldameer's Figure Eight

The "Figure Eight" wooden roller coaster at Waldameer Park is depicted in this 1920s postcard. The roller coaster, designed by Fredrick Ingersoll, debuted at the park in 1907 and closed in 1937. The Great Depression, which began in 1929, was the most influential event that happened in the development of the young amusement park industry. According to the U.S. Census Bureau, in 1930, there were 1,800 to 2,000 amusement parks in America. By 1935, there were only 303 and, by 1939, only 249 were in operation. Fortunately, Waldameer Park was one of the survivors. The Comet at Waldameer Park, which is still in operation today, was built in 1951. *(Postcard submitted by Raymond Groters, historical information from www.ultimaterollercoaster.com).*

Wood farmers

The Wood family poses in their Harborcreek field for this 1927 photo. Pictured are: George Wood (behind tractor), James Wood, Glenn Wood (on tractor) and Helen Wood Schilling. Acting as land agent for the Pennsylvania Population Company, Thomas Rees surveyed much of the Harborcreek area in the late 1790s. However, Harborcreek was not established as a township until 1803. Many of the township's residents were farmers and farming is still an important part of Harborcreek's economy today. *(Donated to the Harborcreek Historical Society by Carol Wood).*

Britain's George Washington?

This statue of George Washington, located on Route 19 in Waterford, is the only statue of him in a British Uniform. As a major representing the Governor of Virginia, Washington visited Waterford in 1753 bearing a letter to the Commander of the fort warning the French to withdraw their forces from the region as it had been claimed by Great Britain. The statue was erected in 1922 upon the site of the original Fort LeBoeuf, in the middle of Route 19 (as shown in this photo). It was later moved to the side in the late 1940s after becoming a traffic hazard. *(Submitted by the Fort LeBoeuf Historical Society).*

Family outing

Charlotte (Weiss) and husband, Jesse Hough, pose with their two children, Dorothy and Leroy in this 1925 photo. The family is shown on an outing to the lot they had just purchased on East 33rd Street in Erie. They paid $50 for the lot which was made, in payments, to the Andrews Land Co. The car was a used one, and the roof leaked in the back where the children rode. They kept an umbrella in the car that the children opened and used in the backseat when it rained. Dorothy later married Harry Latimer and they resided in Fairview most of their lives. *(Submitted by Roger, son of Dorothy Hough Latimer, and Nancy Latimer).*

Maker of Boots and Shoes. 2513 Peach. St. Erie. Pa

IF YOU DONT SEE WHAT YOU WANT FOR IT.

If the shoe fits

John Schenk, right, looks at the camera for this 1920s shot of his shoe store at 2513 Peach St. The business was later moved to the 2500 block of Parade Street. *(Submitted by Rosemary Mangold Teets, John's granddaughter).*

Young musicians

Gathered here are children in a 1926 music class at what is believed to be Lawrence Park Elementary School. The first boy on the far left is Vic Mayer Sr., who went on to be a prominent engineer at General Electric and later, Hammermill Papers. *(Submitted by Elsie Mayer, wife of Vic Mayer).*

"Mad" Anthony's tale

Anna Wojciechowski is shown in front of the Anthony Wayne Blockhouse in this 1927 photo. For a number of years, Anna, her husband, Andrew Regruth and their daughter, Nancy, lived near the blockhouse on Fifth and Reed streets. The blockhouse was reconstructed on the site of French Fort Presque Isle at Second and Ash streets and is named after Revolutionary War hero "Mad" Anthony Wayne who died at the blockhouse and was buried beneath the flagpole until his son, Isaac, came to Erie in 1809 to take his father's remains to Philadelphia. When exhumed, Wayne was found to be perfectly preserved. Isaac Wayne asked a local doctor to deal with the problem. Unknown to Isaac, the doctor boiled the flesh off the bones in a cauldron and re-interred the flesh at the blockhouse. He then gave the bones to Isaac to bury in Philadelphia. The cauldron that Anthony Wayne was boiled in is displayed at the local historical museum in Erie. Therefore, Wayne has the illustrious title of being the only American general buried in two places. *(Submitted by Nancy Regruth Latimer of Fairview, Anna's daughter).*

Tasty treats

These two photos show the inside of the two establishments run by Michael Vicos on the ground floor of the Central Hotel Building at 1218 Peach St. in the late 1920s. One side of the building was a restaurant and the other side of the building was a coffee shop/ice cream parlor. Pictured in the ice cream parlor photo are: (l-r) Michael Vicos, Garaflie Vicos, Charlie Benze, Helen (Vicos) Manos. Michael and Garaflie Vicos had eight children – Mary, Cora, Helen, Katie, Cleo, Teddy, Bessie and Bill. *(Submitted by Cleopatra Vicos Fontecchio).*

Childcraft classmates

Erie area mothers pose with their children in front of the Visiting Nurse Association's office at 319 W. 8th St. in 1928. The women had gathered to attend a "childcraft" class that was conducted by the VNA nurses. At these clinics, the babies and children were given a complete physical examination and the mothers were taught how to keep their babies well and strong. *(Submitted by the Visiting Nurse Association)*.

Mercyhurst memories

In 1926, Mercyhurst College opened its doors on a wind-swept hill overlooking Lake Erie, just a few blocks from the city's southern boundary. The all-women college was founded by the Sisters of Mercy of the Erie Catholic Diocese who put their own sweat and tears into the campus which prospered under the strong leadership of Mother M. Borgia Egan, the college's first president. The heritage of Mercyhurst, however, can be traced back to Mother Catherine McAuley, who founded the Sisters of Mercy in Dublin, Ireland. From the beginning, attention was paid to not just the inside, but also the outside of the college. Old Main, created by architect F. Ferdinand Durang of Philadelphia, became a masterpiece of English Gothic design that is still in use today. During its evolution from acres of farmland to today's modern coed campus, Mercyhurst has undergone dynamic change. In 2003, Mercyhurst covers six city blocks, boasts of 50 buildings and the grounds are one of the most beautiful areas in the region. *(Photos courtesy of the Sister Mary Lawrence Franklin Archives at Mercyhurst College and the archives of the Erie Sisters of Mercy).*

Graduates plant a tree

Mercyhurst College graduates help to plant the Charter Oak on campus. *(Photos courtesy of the Sister Mary Lawrence Franklin Archives at Mercyhurst College and the archives of the Erie Sisters of Mercy).*

Meet the meat marketers

The Przybyszewski brothers, Benny (far left) and Anthony (in the middle) pose in front of their Family Meat Market stand at the Twelfth Street Market in this 1920s era photo. Pictured (l-r) are: Benny Przybyszewski, Clara Przybyszewski Zdunski, Anthony "Tony" Przybyszewski, Alice Miluszewski Przybyszewski and Irene Przybyszewski Bojarski. The brothers were partners in the business and serviced the Erie School District as well as many of Erie's finest restaurants including Tony's and the Erie Restaurant. Benny went on to own a meat market on 13th and Reed streets and Tony continued to run the meat market at the Twelfth Street Market and moved to the Central Market when the Twelfth Street Market was destroyed by fire. *(Submitted by Bernard Przybyszewski, son of Benny).*

Shoe crew

Leo DeMartino (left) and Dominic Italia (right) pose in their shoe repair shop at 26th and Parade streets in this Sept. 1922 photo. The two were partners in the business. According to the photo contributor, the area was once known as "Marvintown" and Dominic, who was well known in the area, was called the "Mayor of Marvintown" and his shop known as the "Marvintown Shoe Repair Shop." Dominic and his wife, Florence, had five children. *(Submitted by Carmen Italia, Dominic's son)*.

Death of the depression

George J. Geiger Sr. drives a float down State Street in a parade celebrating the end of the Great Depression. The epitaph on the monument reads, "Old Man Depression – Born 1929 – Died 1933. Gone but not forgotten." Geiger & Sons, makers of fine monuments and memorials, was established in 1923 by George's father, John A. Geiger, and has remained a family-owned business ever since with third and fourth generation family members operating the business today. *(Submitted by Geiger & Sons Monuments)*.

Red Cross orchestra

World War I found the McKean Chapter of the American Red Cross busy meeting the needs of the servicemen and community. Besides knitting, sewing and rolling bandages, they found time to form a community orchestra under the direction of Steve Blonigan. *(Submitted by Libby Munson-Kramer).*

Partners in meat

Albert "Bert" Dennington and Floyd Irwin stand in the doorway of Bowman & Co. Groceries and Meats on Main Street in downtown Waterford in this c. 1929 photo. The store was owned by Jessie Bowman (shown in the front left in the photo at right) and Bert Dennington who were partners in the business. The building is still standing today and is now a beauty shop. *(Submitted by Helen Breitweiser, daughter of Jessie Bowman).*

"State-of-the-art" canning room

Shown in the photo above is a "canning room" at the country estate of Erie resident, Thomas W. Smith. It is unclear what year this photo was taken, but it was taken by Scobell-Winston Company workers who installed the state-of-the-art plumbing and heating in the room. *(Submitted by Scobell Company Inc.)*

Linemen line-up

Linemen for the Erie County Electric Company (predecessor to Penelec), pose in front of one of their service trucks for this 1928 photo. The only man identified in this photo is Frank Mangold (top row, fifth from right), a lineman and father of two children – Rosemary and Gilbert. *(Submitted by Rosemary Mangold Teets, Frank's daughter).*

Erie's old high school

Old Erie High School, located at West 11th and Sassafras streets was built in 1891. It was called Central School because there was some opposition to spending so much money on just a high school so some grade school classes were held there. By 1907, the graduating class numbered 107 and total enrollment was 874, but it was growing rapidly. In ten years, the graduating class numbered 250. This postcard depicts the school when looking from he corner of 11th and Sassafras to the north. The tower to the left was a challenge to each class coming in. Many young men risked their lives to paint the class number on the roof of that tower. Later this school became Technical High School and was torn down around 1969. *(Submitted by Larry Hubiak, Class of 1955).*

Hard work, respect spell success for Scobell

Scobell & Winston Company, an early Erie plumbing and heating company, was established as a partnership in 1900 and was originally located at 2027 State St. in Erie where it remained until 1959 when it relocated to 220 E. Eighth St. and later, to it's present location at 1256 E. 12th St. Shown in the photo at left is the storefront of the Scobell & Winston Company and, below, is a picture of the interior showroom. In 1946, the company was reorganized as a corporation and renamed Scobell Company, Inc. Mr. Gilbert L. Scobell was the founding partner and president from 1900-1959.

Mr. Scobell started the business with his partner, Mr. George Winston, when he was 19 years old. In 1933, the Carrier Corporation offered a distributorship to Scobell Company, one of only 17 companies in the U.S. to receive this offer. The company was founded on Mr. Scobell's philosophy that anyone who serves their customers with respect, dedicates their time and works hard can achieve their dreams. By following this philosophy, the Scobell Company - specializing in air conditioning, heating, plumbing, industrial piping, ventilating and sheet metal – has grown for over 102 years. *(Submitted by Scobell Company Inc.).*

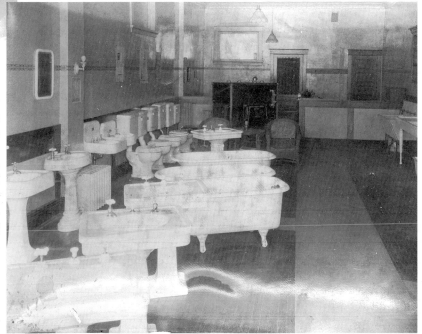

The Turbulent Thirties
1930-1939

Depression marked the 1930s both in Erie and throughout the nation. But, it was also the decade that Gannon University was founded, The Warner Theatre was completed and the first drive-in movie theaters open.

● An act making the "Star-Spangled Banner" the national anthem is signed into law by President Hoover in 1931.

● Amelia Earhart lands in Northern Ireland, becoming the first woman to fly solo across the Atlantic on May 21, 1932.

● The Warner Theatre opens on April 10, 1931 welcoming all of society's players through its doors. That night, the feature film was "The Millionaire".

● The Great Depression forces people to stand in bread lines across a demoralized country, a total of 1,616 U.S. banks fail, nearly 20,000 businesses go bankrupt and U.S. industrial production falls to a third of its 1929 total. Nearly everyone is affected by the Depression, but the poorest Americans suffered most of all.

● FDR suspends banking for several days in the spring of 1933 in an attempt to stop panicking citizens who are withdrawing all their money. When the panic begins, there are 10 banks in Erie — only four will survive the depression.

● Prohibition ends at midnight on Jan. 1, 1934 after 13 years under the 18th Amendment.

● Sarah A. Reed, Erie's "Grand Old Lady" — one of the few who could stand with one foot in society's circles of the rich and educated and one foot in the lives of women and children in need — dies in Dec. of 1934 leaving in her memory two mainstays of Erie's service community — the Sarah A. Reed Children's Center and the Sarah A. Reed Retirement Center.

● Erie's last streetcar (No. 171) makes its final run in May of 1935. Sleek new buses owned by Erie Coach Co. take to the streets the next day. Streetcars had rolled through Erie for 46 years.

● Fire destroys two giant waterfront freight sheds owned by the Pennsylvania Railroad; $400,000 dollars in losses are reported. In addition to obliterating the buildings. The fire destroys 32 freight cars and the merchandise in them.

● Airport expansion begins in Erie in 1936.

● The second of two odd fires at Waldameer Park — the Crazy House and Rainbow Gardens — in 1938 confirms fire department suspicions that an arsonist is at work.

● In December of 1938, General Electric produces the first electric locomotive after nearly two years of effort. When GE puts the diesel-electric locomotive on display, 10,000 visitors get a look at it.

● A terrible winter storm does thousands of dollars worth of damage to the peninsula and Peninsula Road on Dec. 27 in 1938. Photos show eerie frozen landscapes, trees twisted by storm winds and captured in ice. Bulkheads built to protect the peninsula from crashing Lake Erie waves succumb to the storm, leaving the park's road exposed to the lake's water. Eventually, a two-foot tall barrier forms naturally and protects the peninsula. Nearly two feet of ice covers the peninsula highway.

● Classic films "The Wizard of Oz" and "Gone With the Wind" are released.

Boy Scout troop group

St. Mary's Church at Ninth and German streets was quite a prosperous parish in the early 1930s when this photo was taken. Posing in front of the church are the participants in the Boy Scout/Cub Scout Father and Son Communion Breakfast in the spring of 1934. *(Submitted by Gene Kiehlmeier).*

57

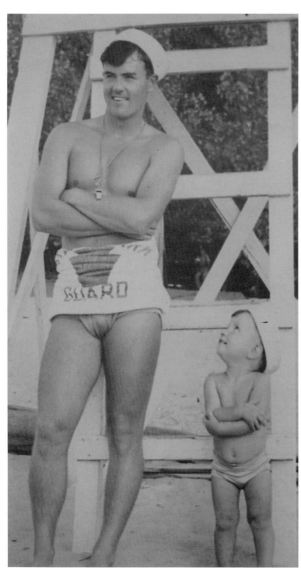

Checkmate

A chess tournament takes place in the lobby of the Downtown Erie YMCA in this c. 1930s photo. Many people believe the YMCA to be an original American concept, but it was actually started in London, England in 1844. It first came to the United States in 1851 with the establishment of the first American YMCA in Boston, Mass. The Downtown Erie YMCA was built in 1911. *(Submitted by the YMCA of Greater Erie).*

Muscle beach

A young boy looks up to a YMCA lifeguard in this c. 1930s photo. Erie, Pa. was one of the earliest supporters of the YMCA movement, establishing the first Erie YMCA on August 27, 1860. The organization's stated goals were to "provide for the religious and social needs of young men." Upon formation, the YMCA boasted 155 members. *(Submitted by the YMCA of Greater Erie).*

Down on the farm

This aerial photo of the Nellis Farm, located at Young Road and Cherry Street Extension (where the Cobblestone Village and Southland Village subdivisions are now located) was taken in 1958. The dairy farm was purchased by John Nellis in 1860 and was in operated by the Nellis family for over 100 years. All of the original buildings are now gone. *(Submitted by Lawrence Nellis).*

Baby buggy

Mary Alice Nellis, 9 months old, is shown in this 1937 photo with her family's farm in the background. This photo was taken looking north on Cherry Street from the Millcreek-Summit Township line. *(Submitted by Lawrence Nellis, brother of Mary Alice).*

Sharpshooters

Depicted in this 1937 photo is Girard's only Rifle Team that participated in a variety of sharpshooting tournaments, competitions and events in the Erie area. The team included: front row, (l-r) Robert Kaehler, Ralph McCray, Earl Hossman, Tom Kuharsky; second row (l-r), Paul Eggleston, Walter Hossman, Merle Mohney, Paul Kuharsky. Earl Hossman is the only rifleman ever inducted into the Erie chapter of the Pennsylvania Sports Hall of Fame (inducted in 1997). *(Submitted by Earl Hossman).*

Paving the way

Dunn Valley Road in McKean was one of the first roads to be converted from gravel to "soil-cement" by the Pennsylvania Department of Highways (PennDOT predecessor). In this 1930s photo, PDH workers are shown converting the road by mixing soil with dry cement and watering it. *(Submitted by William Sachse from the Wesley Moore collection).*

Men of Prep

The graduating class of Cathedral Prep in 1939, pictured here, still get together once a month at the East Erie Turners Club for lunch. Photo contributor, Gene Kiehlmeier, is the fifth boy (from left) in the second row. Pictured with the graduates is Archbishop John Mark Gannon. *(Submitted by Gene Kiehlmeier).*

"Fun Reigns Supreme"

The Bavarian Hofbrau at Waldameer Park "joy spot of Erie, Pa." in the 1930s was "where fun reigns supreme," according to the postcard at left. Unfortunately, it burned down in the 1940s.

In this photo, Hofbrau workers are gathered together for a meal. One of the cooks at the Hofbrau was Helen Aleksa, last woman in the row on the left, who was once offered $500 (which was a lot of money in the 1930s) for her batter recipe by a Duncan Hines worker who ate at the Hofbrau. According to her son, Fr. Thomas Aleksa, Helen politely declined and her recipe remains a secret to this day. *(All three photos submitted by Fr. Thomas Aleksa, son of Helen).*

The Hofbrau was owned by the Hofbrau family pictured above which included – Bertha, Mike, Fritz, Evelyn, Ella, Ella's mother, Evelyn and Chris.

Icy exploration

Margaret Wynne Habermann and her son, Richard Wynne, explore the icy landscape at Presque Isle in 1937. *(Submitted by Richard Wynne).*

Radioland crooners

Amos and Chet Church were local musicians who had a weekly radio show on WLEU AM 1450 in the late 1930s. Here they are shown doing their show in 1937 in the station's studio. Both had day jobs as well. Chet, on the left, is the founder of Erie's Church and Murdock Electric Company and Amos, on the right, worked at Keystone Coat, Apron, and Towel Supply Company. *(Submitted by Karen Clement, granddaughter of Amos).*

Fresh fish

Elmer Edward Hake checks out the "catch of the day" at the Erie Public Dock in these 1937 photos. The sign in the photo above lists "Blue Pike, Perch, Whitefish and Fillets of All Kinds!" In the

bottom photo, fishing nets are shown drying on giant racks. Elmer was married to Gertrude Browning Hake and moved to Erie from Bellevue, Kentucky around the time this photo was taken. They lived on East 21st Street and had four children - Marge, Ruth, Charles and Donald. Elmer worked as a printer at Erie Lithograph. *(Submitted by Nancy Hersch, daughter of Charles).*

Kennedy campaign stop

The Hotel Lawrence, once located at the corner of West 10th and Peach streets was one of the finest hotels in town and was where John F. Kennedy spoke to Erieites during his 1960s presidential campaign stop. The Hotel was razed in the mid-1960s to make room for the Erie Hilton. Next door to the Lawrence Hotel was the Majestic Theater which was built in 1904 and operated under the name of Perry and Sheas until it was torn down along with the Lawrence Hotel. Many of the leading actors and actresses of the time played at the Majestic and, for many years, the commencement exercises of old Erie High School were held there. Located next to theater was the old W.T. Grant building which eventually burned down in the 1950s. *(Submitted by Debbie and Doug Richardson).*

Just a little pinch

A doctor and nurse from the Visiting Nurse Association inoculate children in this 1930s era photo. The VNA was committed not only to caring for the sick and injured but also to preventing the spread of disease which they accomplished by hosting inoculation clinics such as the one pictured here. *(Submitted by the Visiting Nurse Association).*

You should see the one that got away!

George Stephany shows off the large pike he caught during a 1930s fishing trip in Lake Erie. Blue pike, a sub-species of walleye, became a very popular commercial catch in the 1920s, but disappeared from the lake in the late 1950s and are believed to be extinct. Over-fishing is believed to have been the cause for the decline in Lake Erie's fish population. There were no limits on fish catches and fishing was done year-round. Blue pike, whitefish, lake herring and sturgeon all became scarce from over-fishing. *(Submitted by Mary Theiss, George's granddaughter).*

12th Street repair stop

Poplar Auto Parts on West 12th Street was started 75 years ago by Carl Mayr whose mechanics used to repair cars and trucks right on the street until the police would come and tell them to move. In this photo, taken in the 1930s, you can see a much different West 12th Street – with streetcar tracks running down the middle. The business, now known as Poplar Truck Parts & Service, was expanded, but is still in operation in its original location and is currently being run by Mayr's granddaughter, Jennifer (Durst) Manno. *(Submitted by Jennifer Durst Manno).*

Grand opening celebration

George Weber's Band was the opening entertainment at the grand opening of the Warner Theatre on April 10, 1931. George Weber is to the far left of the photo. In the center of the photo, between the two ladies, is Anthony Savelli, a well-known Erie area musician and bandleader. *(Submitted by Geraldine Oligeri, daughter of Anthony Savelli).*

Breadman brings basket

Ralph Dougan, delivery man for Lauterbach Bakery poses with his delivery basket for this 1930s shot. The Lauterbach Bakery was located at 121-123 E. 21st St. and was believed to have been in operation from 1909 to 1946 when Mr. Lauterbauch went to work at Kinneman Bakery. *(Submitted by Audrey Horton, Ralph's niece).*

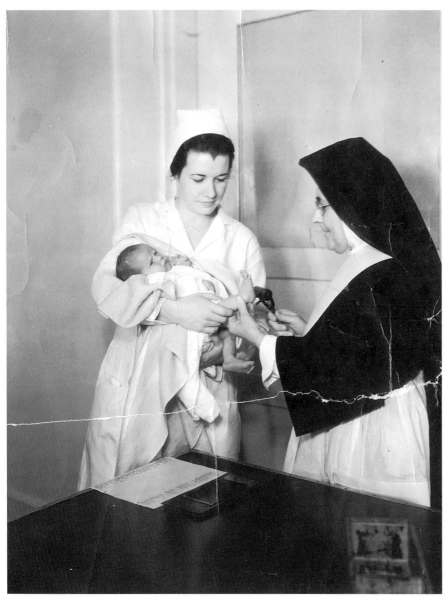

Main street specials

The Fairview Red & White Store was located on Main Street and owned by Jack and Edith Osterberg. This photo shows Jack and Edith's daughter, Evelyn (right) and a neighborhood friend (left) in front of the store in the mid 1930s. Weekly specials are posted on the window – Jell-O gelatin, three boxes for 10 cents; Maxwell House coffee for 25 cents and catsup, two for 23 cents. Note: the neighbor's outhouse in the left side of the photo. *(Submitted by Evelyn Osterberg).*

Foolproof foot printing

Sister Isabel, maternity supervisor at Saint Vincent's hospital, Nurse Alice Nash and baby Gerald Joseph Schillinger demonstrate the newest technology for preventing baby "mix-ups" in the 1930s – foot portraits – an "iron-clad prevention against mistaking baby identities" according to the newspaper article that accompanied this 1933 photo. The article goes on to say that footprinting babies is quite a difficult task as it "is difficult to get their frail little bodies straight and held in that position so the foot can be pressed firmly down on the imprint paper." Today, footprints are just a souvenir for parents due to the development of DNA testing. *(Submitted by Patricia Murphy, LDR nurse at Saint Vincent Health Center).*

Standing tall

Erie area children participate in a "Posture Class" at the Visiting Nurse Association offices at 319 W. Eighth St. in this 1930s photo. The classes, taught by VNA nurses, were intended to help the preschool children develop good posture and fitness. *(Submitted by the Visiting Nurse Association).*

Victory Band

The Erie Works Victory Band is shown in this c. 1940s photo taken in front of the Erie Works Community Center (now the G.E. Museum). The band members' names are at right as listed in their concert program. *(Submitted by Bob Weisenbach, Nephew of band director, Frank Donaldson).*

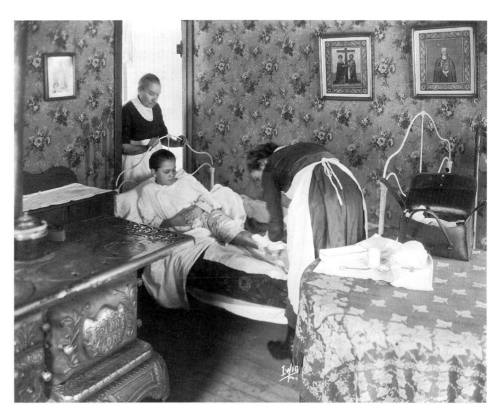

Paying a visit

This 1930s photo illustrates a typical home visit by a Visiting Nurse Association nurse who would go to the home to care for, and show family members how to care for, the sick and injured. By this time in history, the VNA had cared for 32 families during the Mill Creek Flood of 1915 and engaged 13 extra nurses during the World War I flu epidemic. They had also started child health stations staffed by two nurses and had undertaken selection and supervision of children for the newly established Kiwanis Camp. *(Submitted by the Visiting Nurse Association).*

Night class cooks

This photo, believe to have been taken in the 1920s, depicts a night cooking class at Academy High School. Among the students are Anna Gieringer (Schumacher) and Florence Johnson. *(Submitted by Mildred Shenk, daughter of Anna).*

The snow king!

Pennsylvania Department of Highway (predecessor to PennDOT) employees pose in front of a Walter "snow king" plow in this c. 1930s photo taken at the original garage on the north side of Marsh Street in Erie. The names listed on the back of the photo are: Wes, Louie, Albert, Jackson, Bill, Ara, Hickey, Josh, Mike, Shum and Bill. *(Submitted by William Sachse from the Wesley Moore collection).*

Let me call you sweetheart #29

Sweetheart Couple #29 Sally Regan and Eddie Bush pose for this c. 1930s photo at Terrace Gardens at Waldameer Park. The Terrace Gardens later burned down and was replaced by the current Rainbow Gardens. The couple pictured here were participants in a dance marathon competition at the gardens. *(Submitted by Gertrude Washok).*

Tech school swimmers

One of the standouts on the Tech High School swim team in the mid 1930s was Zigmund "Whitey" Dobrowolski (at right). Whitey was never beaten in high school competition in any event and held the world's record in the 100 yard freestyle. He led Tech to the state championship in 1935 by winning the 220 yard freestyle while also winning the 40 and 100 yard freestyles. He also won the national meet and was a PIAA official for almost 30 years. At left is a Tech High Swim Team photo from the 1936-37 school year. The last names of the men pictured (l-r) are: Dobrowolski (team captain), Ostromecki, Zielonka, Sackett, Visnoski, Dlugas, Seyler, Welka, Bebko, Schoeller, Kelly, Nelson, Kostek, B. Strand, A. Strand, Haglund and Manager. *(Submitted by Toni Dobrowolski, daughter of "Whitey" Dobrowolski).*

VNA provides TLC

VNA (Visiting Nurse Association) nurse, Ann Koehler, RN conducts a home visit in this 1938 photo. The nurse would examine the baby, answer any of the mother's questions and show the mother how to care for the infant. *(Submitted by the Visiting Nurse Association).*

Out for a stroll

Jeanette Bruce, wife of Joseph G. Bruce Sr., pushes her daughter, Barbara, down State Street in this 1935 photo. At that time, the Bruce's lived in an upstairs apartment above Washington Cleaners on State Street. *(Submitted by Barbara Bruce Gaeckle).*

Bargain lunch choices

The New Post Office Lunch, located at 1218 Peach St. (where WSEE is now located) in the Central Hotel was operated by Michael Vicos who is shown standing in front of the building in this 1930s photo with his daughter, Cleopatra. According to Cleopatra, the restaurant offered bargain meals during the depression — for 10 cents lunch patrons got bread, butter, soup, coffee, meat, vegetable and potatoes. For two cents they could purchase a small piece of pie and, for five cents, they could get a regular slice of pie or coffee and two donuts. Breakfast included three hotcakes, butter and syrup for five cents. Ham, bacon or sausage was an additional five cents. *(Submitted by Cleopatra Fontecchio).*

Advancing technology

Amazing technological and electrical advances have been made since these students in the field of Electrical Construction at Erie Technical High School are shown at work in this mid 1930s photo. The class instructor was Claude McNally and the students pictured here include: (last names only) Coudriet, Perry, Hain, Rutkowski, Brzozowski, Kaday, Hagmann, Juchno, Czuprynski, Schaack and Bedner. *(Submitted by Toni Dobrowolski).*

Holy Cow!

People often walk their dogs, but how often do you see someone taking their cow for a stroll? In this 1931 photo, Olive Spratt, Margaret Walker and Mr. Beson are shown at the corner of East Normal and High streets in Edinboro walking from the pasture (now Edinboro University on High Street) to Mr. Beson's barn behind his house on High Street. In the background of the photo, you can see Academy Hall and the houses on East Normal Street (where EUP's Compton Hall is now located). *(Submitted by Margaret Walker).*

Store celebrates golden anniversary

The W. T. Grant Co. Department Store was located on the northwest corner of 10th and State streets where the Avalon Hotel now stands. This photo was taken in 1932 when the company was celebrating the 50th anniversary of the W.T Grant Co. which was founded in 1882. Store Manager, Ralph Brucker, is in the center of the photo. The other men in the photo, called "floor walkers," were assistant managers. The photo contributor's mother, Mary Benacci, is located in the middle of the first row in the white v-neck dress. Mary worked in the jewelry department and later in small pets. She worked Monday through Friday from 9-6 and Saturdays from 9-9 and earned $9 a week. At that time, there was no vacation, no holiday pay and no sick time, but Mary said her mother was grateful to have a job when so many were out of work during the depression. *(Submitted by Mary Benacci).*

Lovell Building baby

Dorothia Wright poses with family friend, Gwen King (baby sitting on car) in front of the Lovell Building in this 1930s photo. The Lovell complex once housed the largest manufacturer of hand-cranked wringer washers in the world. It went out of business in the 1970s. Now known as Lovell Place, the building has been renovated into retail space, business offices and residential apartments. *(Submitted by Ruth Ranson, Gwen's cousin).*

Plavcan's proteges

Erie Technical High School Art students are shown working on an assignment in this c. 1936 photo. The instructor was Joseph Plavcan, a well-known and much revered Erie artist and painter who died in 1981. The last names of the students pictured are: Tannenbaum, Evans, Waldinger, Woodring, Tillman, Strohmeyer, Kunik, Dishinger, Hultgren, Aitken, Shroup, Kaminski, Garries, Chamberlain and Traczenski. *(Submitted by Toni Dobrowolski).*

Secret sweethearts have a second wedding

High school sweethearts, Bill Jant and Eva Hartmann, are shown in this 1931 photo taken in Bill's mother's rose garden on East Seventh Street just before the two eloped. Eva was a Catholic and Bill was raised Lutheran and, in those days, interfaith marriages were not condoned by parents. So, on a beautiful fall day in September of 1931, they took the Buffalo streetcar to Ripley where they were married by a justice of the peace. Their secret was kept until the following year when Eva's sister, Clara, "accidentally" found their marriage license, buried under the paper lining of her dresser drawer. The result was another wedding – this time at the rectory of St. Ann's Catholic Church on May 7, 1932. The two went on to have three daughters – Charlotte, Beverly and Barbara. *(Submitted by Beverly Pochatko, daughter).*

1931

Abbate's eastside grocery

Antonio Abbate was the proprietor of this corner grocery store, Nino Abbate's Grocery, Meat & Produce, at Fourth and German streets, show in this 1931 photo. The store served eastside Erie residents from 1928 to 1978. *(Submitted by Frank Abbate, son of Antonio Abbate).*

Picture perfect wedding portrait
This wedding portrait depicts the marriage of Rose Isabelle Hoffman and Joseph Cyril Wittman on June 24, 1936.
Attendants were: (l-r) Madeline Yaeger, James Adrian Wittman and Irene Hoffman. Flowergirls are Marilyn and Marlene
Hoffman. *(Submitted by Mary Pope, daughter of Rose and Joseph Wittman).*

Thinking inside the box

In this photo, boys at the YMCA's Camp Sherwin square off for a game of "box hockey." First established in 1912, Camp Sherwin is still a great place for kids of all ages. The camp offers cabins, swimming pool, nature trails, an inland pond for boating, beach access, ball fields, basketball and much more. *(Submitted by the YMCA of Greater Erie).*

Stadler's celebrate 60 years of marriage

John J. and Rose (Seus) Stadler – shown here in this 1936 photo taken on the occasion of their 60th wedding anniversary – owned a large farm on the corner of Lake Pleasant and Sampson Road (then known as Wolf Road) where they had twelve children. They worked as farmers and grew a variety of produce that they would sell at the fruit market in Erie. John was born in Bavaria, Germany in 1852 and came to the U.S. when he was about 20 years old. According to his grandson, he was one of the first men to own a motorcar in Greene township. Until he had an accident, that is. After that, he never drove again. The original homestead is still standing and is owned by the Burbles family. *(Submitted by Paul Stadler, grandson of John and Rose).*

The Fabulous Forties
1940-1949

Erie confronted war, rationing, fire and coal strikes in the 1940s. It was also the decade that Hamot Hospital and Saint Vincent Hospital opened and the decade that saw the installation of parking meter, overhead traffic lights and paralyzing snowstorms.

● Saint Vincent Hospital annex is dedicated on Jan 1, 1940.

● In the first of what will be several spectacular snowstorms in the decade, a record snowfall shuts the city down (Feb., 1940).

● The first of many Erie city streets are converted to one-way: Seventh, Eighth and Ninth streets between Liberty and Parade streets.

● "A Day that will live in infamy" – Dec. 7, 1941 - the U.S. was suddenly and deliberately attacked by naval and air forces of the Empire of Japan in a raid on the Pearl Harbor naval base in Hawaii. The attack kills 2,330 servicemen and 100 civilians. Sgt. Anthony Restivao, 26, of West 17th Street, is Erie's first war casualty.

● On Dec. 11, 1941, Hitler declares war on the U.S., an action that seals his fate and ensures the defeat of the Axis powers.

● The city and county agree to fund the first blood bank in Erie; start-up costs are $6,310.

● Rationing – beginning with tires and gasoline – begins in Erie in 1942. Shoes, milk, meat and potatoes are among the hot commodities in the city as supplies dwindle (1943).

● In 1945, restaurants adopt a new meatless Tuesday and Friday menus as the meat shortage grows more severe.

● Two Erie firefighters are killed as a disastrous fire destroys the Isaac Baker store in downtown Erie on Dec. 11, 1941.

● Seventy German prisoners-of-war arrive at Camp Reynolds in North East to help in canneries on June 14, 1944.

● The Army sends in troops in an effort to break Erie from the winter storms that have battered the area for nearly a month. It takes 450 soldiers, their trucks and plows to battle the record snowfall (Jan. 1945).

● On Aug. 6, 1945, a new weapon called "the atomic bomb" is dropped on Hiroshima, Japan, leading to the surrender of Japan and Germany and ending a six-year global war that left 55 million people dead.

● Hamot Hospital announces a $1.8 million expansion plan. The new 10-story structure will house 483 beds plus a new surgery department, a maternity ward, an X-ray department. and an outpatient area (Nov. 1945).

● The City of Erie approves installation of parking meters (Dec. 5, 1945).

● Production ceases at the Erie Works of General Electric Co., when 6,100 members of the United Electrical, Radio and Machine Workers Union go on strike in Jan. of 1946.

● Erie is among those areas that are "browned out" after 6 p.m., the result of the continuing coal strike and subsequent shortage of fuel. Twenty-one states are impacted.

● Construction of a Veteran's hospital begins (1948).

● City council decides to retain overhead traffic lights (1949).

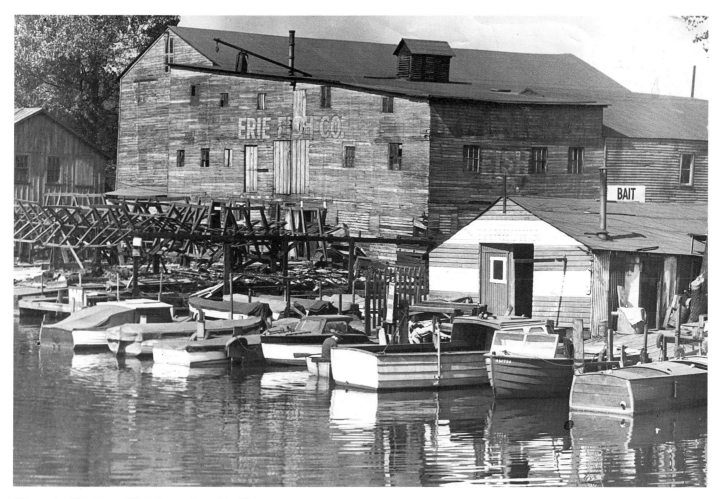

"Fresh Water Fishing Capital"

This 1940s shot of Erie's bayfront shows the Erie Fish Co. and Smitty's Bait Stand at the foot of State Street. Photo contributor, John S. Balkovic, remembers playing in this area with his friends when he was a child and says the water was so clear you could see the bass swimming around your feet. According to John, the wooden racks in left side of the photo were used for drying fish nets. At its peak in the 1920s, over 140 fishing tugs steamed out of Erie's harbor, bringing their catch back to the city's 14 fish processing plants. Commercial fishing was a million-dollar-a-year industry, employing 3,500 men full-time. In 1920, the Chamber of Commerce proclaimed Erie the "Fresh Water Fishing Capital of the World." By the late 1990s, however, Erie's commercial fishing fleet had dwindled down to just a few boats and is now virtually non-existent. The area shown here is now occupied by the Waterfront Restaurant. *(Submitted by John S. Balkovic)*.

Historic Wolverine

Pictured here is the Wolverine – the first iron-clad ship of the U.S. Navy – before it was hauled away to be scrapped in 1949. In the photo at right, Stanley and Helen Aleksa pose with friends aboard the crumbling ship. Stanley, a welder by trade, who also sailed for Erie Sand & Gravel, would later help to tow the ship to the scrapyard. The Wolverine has been a part of Erie's history for over 100 years. Because of this ship, first known at the U.S.S. Michigan, Erie was known as the mother-in-law of the Navy because the young crews coming to town met the young ladies of Erie and many were married. Work was started on the ship at the foot of French Street in 1843. The iron plates and parts were made ready for assembly in Pittsburgh and hauled by ox team through the forests to Erie. It was a paddle wheel, bark rigged steamer that sailed the lakes for 80 years. All that is left of it now is the prow which is located at the Erie Maritime Museum. *(Submitted by Fr. Thomas Aleksa, son of Stanley Aleksa).*

Photos for soldiers

These four photos are from a wallet-size leather album that was put together by the Belle Valley Ladies Auxiliary and mailed to Belle Valley area soldiers recuperating in military hospitals during World War II. The photos from this album were sent to Sgt. Robert Connaroe, a Marine who was injured in Guadalcanal and recuperating in a U.S. Naval Hospital in Oakland, California in 1942. *(Submitted by Laura Jean Karle and Dave Connaroe, Robert's wife and son).*

The J.A. Holtz Garage, shown at left, is still located on Norcross Road at the foot of Martin Road.

The Belle Valley Grange.

Pictured here is the Belle Valley Presbyterian Church on Norcross Road which is still in use today.

The "Red & White" Food store is shown above. The woman on the far right is Laura Jean Karle who Sgt. Robert Connaroe (the man who received this album) would eventually marry (though he did not know her at the time this photo was taken or sent to him).

Inside Abbate's

Antonio Abbate, far right in apron, is shown here with employees (three of whom are his children) in 1946 at his food market located on Fourth and German streets in downtown Erie. Pictured (l-r) are: Hank Wienczkowski (head butcher); Joe Abbate, Mamie Abbate; Peter Abbate and Antonio Abbate. Antonio had six children – five boys and one girl – Joe, Peter, Mamie, Frank, Russel and John. *(Submitted by Frank Abbate, son of Antonio Abbate).*

Mother and daughter DeCosta

Helen and daughter, Nancy, DeCosta pose outside their apartment (above an old Chinese laundry) on Fifth and State streets in downtown Erie in this 1947 photo. Helen had four daughters – Mary, Helen, Alberta and Nancy. Nancy says that the State Street area was her "playground" when she was growing up and there was always plenty to do and lots of other children to play with. *(Submitted by Nancy DeCosta Dash).*

Under maintenance

This photo was taken in the 1940s in the maintenance bays of the Erie Coach Co. (predecessor to the EMTA) at their old location on the west side of State Street between Second and Third streets. *(Submitted by Bill Alloway).*

Times Bantam football boys

The Times Bantam football league included this rough and tumble group of boys from Erie's east side. Taken in the early 1940s in front of the old Liberty Club on East 26th Street in Erie, Kenneth Massing (first row, second from left) recalls the last names of some of the players included: Sawtelle, Ferretti, Denniston, Nardo, Manucci, Malatesta and Keller. *(Submitted by Kenneth Massing).*

First Girard draftees

Pictured here are the first men drafted into military service from the Girard Area Draft Board. They are: (l-r), Private Fritz Angerer, Private Edward Carter, Private Farley Forbes and Private Tony Disolvo. According to Angerer, the men got on the bus in front of the Girard post office that was, at that time, located next to Fred Wright's Tavern, directly across from the National Bank of Girard at the corner of Wall and Main streets. From there, the men went to Pittsburgh for physicals and induction and they all left the same day for Fort Meade, Md. where they received their clothing and equipment. This photo was taken Feb. 22, 1941 at Ft. Meade just before the men went their separate ways. *(Submitted by Fritz Angerer).*

Need a ride?

Robert "Bob" Steiner, 2, gets a lift from his big brother Kenneth, 16, on his bicycle in this 1943 photo. After this photo was taken, Kenneth quit school to join the navy and fight in World War II. One of the boys' uncles, Edward Steiner, who was living with the boys' grandfather was the Air Raid Warden and had various emergency supplies on hand including masks and other equipment. Apparently, he was responsible for going throughout the neighborhood and warning residents in the case of an air attack. *(Submitted by Bob Steiner).*

Guess who worked for the Erie Coach Co.?

The Erie Coach Co. (predecessor to the Erie Metropolitan Transit Authority) maintenance crew pose for this 1944 photo. The contributor's father is Bill Alloway Sr. – titled "Guess Who?" – in the last row, on the right. (*Submitted by Bill Alloway, son of Bill Alloway Sr.*)

S'no way a car will get through here!

This photo, marked "Hornby South" in Erie County, is believed to be what is now the intersection of Williams and Station Roads near the old Hornby School in Greenfield Township. This photo, taken in 1945, shows what the rural roads looked like before the plows came through. *(Photo submitted by William Sachse from the Wesley Moore collection)*.

A taste of Italy

The Randazzo name has a rich history in the Erie restaurant scene. This photo, c. 1947, shows Peter Randazzo in his establishment, Randazzo's Tavern, at 701 W. 11th St. which was in operation from 1947-1957. Peter and his wife, Rose, went on to open Randazzo's Restaurant at Eighth and Myrtle streets (photo at right) which quickly became a popular spot with Erie diners looking for authentic Italian cuisine.

(Submitted by Frank Randazzo, son of Peter Randazzo).

100 year schoolhouse

This circa 1844 one-room school house on South Creek Road in Girard was used as a school house for approximately 100 years. It was known as the Globe School in the 1900s, but may also have been known as Blair School in the 1800s. The famous actor, Denman Thompson, lived nearby and might have been among the school's first students. *(Submitted by Mark Sakuta, who now lives in the old Globe school building).*

Old-time grocery

Shown in this photo is a typical 1940s era grocery store. This particular store, owned by Nick Sementilli, was located as 1202 W. 20th St. Mr. Sementilli came from Italy through Ellis Island when he was sixteen years old. *(Submitted by Patricia Rihel, daughter of Nick Sementilli).*

Cheapest gas in town

Hossman Motor Sales – Pontiac – GMC Trucks, owned by Earl Hossman, was a fixture on the corner of Main and Chestnut streets in Girard for years. This photo, taken in 1940 shows the price of gas as 13 cents a gallon! According to Hossman, the car in the showroom window is a new 1940 Pontiac that sold for $940. *(Submitted by Earl Hossman).*

St. Mary's early altar

This 1930s photo shows the inside of St. Mary's Church at Ninth and German streets in Erie. According to the photo contributor, all that remains of this elaborate display after extensive renovation is the altar. *(Submitted by Gene Kiehlmeier, St. Mary's parishioner).*

Casselman – For women only

This photo was on the front of an early real estate sales postcard promoting "The Casselman – Ladies' Apartments" on East Sixth Street in Erie. The apartments, once owned by Rocco and Vincy Cipolla, were advertised at the price of $2 to $3.50 per week and it "was the opinion of all who have inspected the premises that charges were reasonable." Below is the backside of the postcard. *(Submitted by Phyllis Hlavin).*

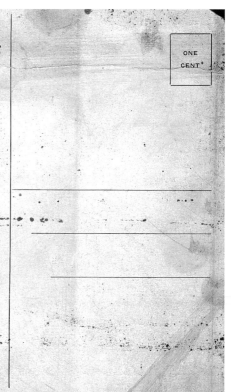

Ladies' Apartments
"THE CASSELMAN"

East Sixth Street, Corner of Lighthouse

Seventy-four rooms, baths, steam heat, electric for lighting, use of grills and irons. Furnished with modern-up-to-date equipment, putting Erie in this particular on a plane with larger cities; will fill the demand of professional and business women.

Price of rooms $2.00 to $3.50 per week. It is the opinion of all who have inspected the premises that charges are very reasonable.

One of the officials of the Y. W. C. A. and the Matron of the General Electric company, are both located in the building and are not only willing, but have expressed a desire to assist in looking after the welfare of the occupants in so far as their counsel and advice may be helpful in making the apartments a desirable home for desirable people.

The building is now open and applications from prospective tenants are being received. Reservations will be made for near future and it is requested you confer with management at your earliest convenience. Office open from 8:30 a. m. to 6:00 p. m., except 12 to 1 noon.

Mutual Realty Company
1172-74 East Sixth St., Corner Lighthouse

Mutual 20-45

ONE CENT

Villa Maria grads

The 1946 graduating class of Villa Maria Academy pose in front of their alma mater on West Ninth Street between Liberty and Plum streets. This building has been turned into senior housing apartments. Photo contributor, Katherine Harmle Kloecker, is shown in the second row from the back, second from the right. *(Submitted by Katherine Harmle Kloecker).*

Frozen Ford

Pennsylvania Department of Highway (predecessor to PennDOT) employees work to free a 1947 Ford stuck in the snow so that the plow can get through. *(Submitted by William Sachse from the collection of Wesley Moore).*

Dashing through the snow

A plow makes its way down what is believed to be Dougan Road about one-half mile south of Station Road in Greene Township in 1945. *(Submitted by William Sachse from the Wesley Moore collection).*

No slip-up

This photo, taken by Ralph Carver in the late 1940s, shows a Water Department boat tied up in the west slip across from the old sand and gravel dock. *(Submitted by Ralph Carver).*

Hog heaven

Farmer, Kenneth N. Lewis, (far left) poses for this mid-1930s photo with his sisters, Irene and Hazel, in one of their family's fields on Old State Road in McLane. *(Submitted by Tammy Podpora, granddaughter of Kenneth Lewis).*

Extra...extra...read all about it!

Charles Hake gets caught up on all the days news by reading the Erie Daily Times in this 1940s photo. Charles was born in Bellevue, Kentucky and worked as a sheet metal worker at General Electric. He was married to Carmella Mobilia Hake (shortly before being shipped out for World War II) and they had four children, Charles, Nancy, Mary Jo and Joseph. *(Submitted by Nancy Hersch, daughter of Charles).*

Erie's "Lakers"

The "Lakers" basketball team played at the old Russian Neighborhood House in 1947 on the corner of Front and German streets in downtown Erie. The last names of the people pictured are: front row – Zydenski, Gregoroff, Spinelli, Biletnikoff; second row – Abatta, Zatkoff, Gomolekoff, (Peter) Alex, Smith and Biletnikoff. Peter Alex went on to start Alex Roofing and, with his wife, Barbara, had four children – Lisa, Peter III, Pamela and Patrick. They currently have 14 grandchildren. *(Submitted by Barbara Alex, wife of Peter Alex II).*

Junior baseball champs

Shown here are the Post No. 11 Junior baseball champs of 1949. The team won 23 games and lost only 5 that season. *(Submitted by Pat Harkins).*

Moo'vin on down the road

Harold and LaVern Vogt pose with their oxen team in this 1940s photo taken at their Barton Road farm. Anton Vogt, who would have been Harold and LaVern's great grandfather, came to Greene Township in 1853 and bought the, then wooded, farm on Barton Road. Anton had eleven children and served in the Civil War and he also helped build the foundation of St. Paul's United Evangelical Church located on Route 8 near the Beechwood Tavern where several of the family members are buried. Today, the Vogt farmland is part of the Pennsylvania Game Commission game lands. *(Submitted by Evelyn Shelhamer, niece of Harold and LaVern).*

No "Fiddle Inn" this band

The old "Fiddle Inn" in Harborcreek was the setting for this 1941 portrait of this three-person band. Band members are (l-r) Harry G. Morgan, Jeanette Wakeley Koskie and Delmar Russel. All three were Harbor Creek High School graduates who were paid to play on Saturday nights for about four hours. Jeanette recalls that, at that time, the Fiddle Inn was located on the north side of Buffalo Road across from the old Johnny Knowles, which is the present-day Fiddle Inn. *(Submitted by Jeanette Koskie).*

Not your typical "gang"

The "Patterson Avenue Gang" consisted of a group of boys who resided in the Patterson Avenue area of Erie and often played together. They even had matching jackets – not as a symbol of their gang membership – but because these "Mackinaw" jackets (named for MacKinaw Island, Michigan) were all the rage during the late 1940s when this photo was taken. The boys are (l-r) Dick Osborne, Bill Jones, Jim Hoffman, Edward "Buzz" Hoffman and Dan Storrer. *(Submitted by Edward "Buzz" Hoffman).*

Patriotic fashion sense

During World War II, dressing children in special military outfits was considered both trendy and patriotic. These boys were proud to display their sailor suits, complete with U.S. Navy caps. The children are siblings, Edward "Buzz" Hoffman, Mary Elaine Hoffman Agnello and James Hoffman and the photo was taken in 1943 at their home on Patterson Avenue *(Submitted by Edward "Buzz" Hoffman).*

1940s Funeral home founder

Gus Dusckas, shown below with his wife, Joan and daughters, Nancy and Connie, was the founder of the Dusckas Funeral Home at 2607 Buffalo Rd. (which now has a second location at 536 W. 10th St.). Gus bought an 1800s era farmhouse on Buffalo Road and developed it into a funeral home in 1946. As the business grew, he began adding onto the original structure – creating various parlors, hallways and offices throughout the years. The original building is now surrounded by newer construction. But, the original wall, windows and woodwork are featured in the interior design of the home. (*Submitted by Nancy Dusckas, daughter of Gus Dusckas and current Funeral Director at Dusckas Funeral Homes*).

Swan pond

Arleen, 5, holds tight to her father, John Tomczak, as he reaches to feed the swans at the Laurel Hill Cemetery on Sterrettania Road. Arlene remembers that they used to go to the cemetery almost every Sunday afternoon in the summer to feed the swans and that she was always quite afraid of them. *(Submitted by Arleen Tomczak Trombetta)*.

The tale of Gudgeonville Bridge

These 1950s photos of the Gudgeonville Bridge were taken by Erie native and avid amateur photographer, Fred Carver (photo at right). The children are unidentified; they simply happened to be playing at the bridge the day that Fred was shooting there. The Gudgeonville Bridge crosses Elk Creek just south of Girard in western Erie County. It has possibly the strangest history of any bridge in the world. In 1855, a Kentuckian named Obadiah Will was delivering a mule named Gudgeon to somebody in Meadville. He stayed overnight in Girard at the old Martin House. When he left the next morning, he was told to follow the road just west of Elk Creek on through Cranesville, which would take him right to Meadville. A couple of miles south, he got off on another road that took him to an unnamed settlement (which later became known as Gudgeonville). It was only a short distance from the covered bridge which spans Elk Creek to the old Beaver and Erie Canal, which was abandoned in 1871. Just as Mr. Will and the mule got on the bridge, a couple of canal boats came up from the south. They carried a circus, and one of the boats was a calliope. The man who operated the calliope began to play a tune — My Old Kentucky Home. Perking up his ears at the weird sound, the animal dug its front hoofs into some planks of the bridge and dropped dead in its tracks. The story was that the mule had been off its feed for several days — lonesome for Kentucky, perhaps. Mr. Will was given permission to bury the mule on the west bank of the creek, and he marked the spot with a large stone. He hired a painter to go out from Girard and paint the word "Gudgeonville" on each end of the bridge. That's how it got the name. When Dan Rice's circus returned to winter quarters at Girard, Dan was told about the mule and the calliope, and he wrote a sad tale of Gudgeon's demise. *(Submitted by Ralph Carver, son of Fred Carver).*

GE worker pride

Workers pose in front of the first Fairbanks-Morse locomotive built for Kansas City at the General Electric plant in Lawrence Park in 1945. Engineer, Victor "Vic" Mayer Sr. is in the first row, second from the right. Vic was a prominent General Electric engineer for 10 years before going to work at Hammermill Papers on East Lake Road. *(Submitted by Elsie Mayer, Vic's wife).*

Diggin' in

Paul (left) and his brother, Fred (right) pose inside their snowfort in this 1940s photo taken at their home on Poplar Street in Erie. According to Paul, the boys would shovel all of the driveway snow and pile it up alongside the garage and tunnel through it. Paul grew up to work at GTE and Fred at General Electric – both are retired now and Fred lives in Florida. *(Submitted by Paul Gaeckle).*

Daddy's girl

Victor Mayer Sr. and his daughter, Gail, clown around at Shade's Beach in Harborcreek in this 1944 photo. *(Submitted by Elsie Mayer, wife of Victor, mother of Gail).*

"Care saves wear"

Leopold's Esso Service Center was located on the corner of State and Orchard streets in downtown Albion. Pictured here is Mr. Kreider, a cousin of the service center owner, Burt Leopold. The service center operated as such until the 1970s when it became an auto parts store and was subsequently destroyed by the Albion tornado in 1985. *(Submitted by Kathy Locke, daughter of Burt Leopold).*

Read Dress Studio workers

The Read Dress Studio, located at 21 W. Ninth St., was a popular shopping destination for women in the 1940s. LaRue Nicholson, a Read's employee and model poses behind the counter in this 1947 promotional photo. The light-haired woman is unidentified. *(Submitted by Tami Carrara, daughter of LaRue).*

Popular Pope Hotel

The Pope Hotel was an extremely popular gathering place located at 14th and French streets. Pictured here in this 1940s photo taken at the Pope Hotel are (l-r): Wendell King, Daddy Jones (believed to be the proprietor of the club), Hannah Wright (whose husband ran the establishment) and Gwendolyn King. Ernie Wright later took over the club until it was closed and destroyed in the late '80s or early '90s, according to photo contributor, Ruth Ranson. In the photo below, Wendell King is seen in his place of business at the Bliley Electric lab. Wendell was an Electrical Engineer who was well-known in the Erie area for his role in developing the intercom system used by taxi cabs and police officers. *(Submitted by Ruth Ranson, cousin of Wendell's wife, Gwen).*

Early bus advertising

City bus driver, Adam Nicholson, poses in front of his bus – advertising War Bonds – stopped in front of Strong Vincent High School in the 1940s. Nicholson later opened Nicholson Restaurant on State Street and then, Adam W. Nicholson Trucking which sold all of the bark in the city of Erie until the 1980s. *(Submitted by Tammi Carrara, daughter of Adam).*

Making the grade

Pictured here the 1944-1945 first grade class at Battles Memorial School in Girard. According to photo contributor, Robert Martin (second row, far right), there were no Kindergarten classes during World War II due to teacher shortages. This class was somewhat unusual because when they entered high school from the eighth grade, the boys outnumbered the girls 20 to 8. The teacher in this photo is Miss Esther Neil who Martin said was a devoted educator in both Girard and North East. The school is now demolished. *(Submitted by Robert B. Martin).*

Keep on rolling

Richard Auer (left) is shown in this 1948 photo demonstrating the "rolling mill" machine that he helped to design and build for General Electric. He was awarded a $27 bonus for building the machine. *(Submitted by Richard Auer).*

Early electronics shop

The Erie Electronics store was located at 18th and Liberty streets and was owned by Elmer Goetz when this photo was taken in the late 1940s. Elmer later went to work at Arthur F. Schultz as an electronics repairman and was one of the first persons in town to repair early microwave ovens. *(Submitted by Cheryl Goetz, daughter-in-law of Elmer Goetz).*

Gleason girls

The Gleason family women pose in front of the old Corry High School building on West Pleasant Street for this 1941 photo. Mother, Thelma, is in the center of the photo holding her daughter, Betty, with daughters, Janey (left) and Norma (right) flanking her. The Gleason family lived across the street from the school. *(Submitted by Mary Ann Granahan, Norma's daughter)*.

Thrasher in action

This 1940s photo shows a "thrashing machine" – used to separate the grain (oats) from the husk – in action at a Union City Farm on Old Meadville Road. The grain would fall into bags and the straw was blown into a big stack which was later used for bedding for cows. *(Submitted by Annie and Louis Sokolowski)*.

Vintage vestments

James Carey poses in his alter boy robes in front of his home at 838 E. 30th St. in this 1941 photo. James served as an altar boy at Holy Rosary Church on East Avenue in Erie. *(Submitted by Kathleen Carey Longley, James' daughter)*.

Old seminary

The Lakeshore Seminary – now Mercyhurst College's North East campus – is shown in this 1949 photo. The seminary was a Methodist and Presbyterian seminary that was purchased in 1881 by the Redemptorist Fathers, who relocated their Catholic St. Mary's Seminary from Baltimore, Md., to North East, Pa. Young men were trained as priests at the seminary for more than a century. Photo contributor, Mary Wheaton, remembers lines of boys who would arrive by train and walk down the road to the seminary in complete silence. The seminary closed in 1987. Its buildings, later including the present-day Newman Hall and a chapel built in 1901, stood empty for four years before Mercyhurst renovated them. *(Submitted by Mary Wheaton).*

Original campus shuttle

Mercyhurst students pose with their school bus in front of "Old Main." *(Photos courtesy of the Sister Mary Lawrence Franklin Archives at Mercyhurst College and the archives of the Erie Sisters of Mercy).*

1st Annual Erie County
Pharmaceutical Picnic 1948

Pharmacists post at picnic

Guests of the First Annual Erie County Pharmaceutical Picnic pose in the backyard of Thieman's Catering (now Stephany's Catering), 1022 Wyoming Ave., in this 1948 photo. The people in this photo were likely local pharmacists, pharmacy employees and their families. *(Submitted by Mary Theiss, current owner of Stephany's Catering, from the George Clark collection).*

Deadly Baker Store blaze

The Isaac Baker & Son Men's Store at 729 State St. caught on fire on Dec. 11 in 1941. Two Erie firefighters, Cletus Hess and George Scully, died while fighting this fire when the north wall fell out (shown in the photo below). The front of the building (looking east from State Street) is shown at left. *(Courtesy of the Firefighters Historical Museum, Inc.).*

Holy portrait

Joseph G. Bruce Jr. poses at St. Joseph's Catholic Church for his First Holy Communion picture taken in 1944. *(Submitted by Heather Cass, Joseph's daughter).*

Winter wedding wonderland

Irene Nolan and her new husband, Paul Canfield, pose in this wintry photo taken on their wedding day – Dec. 12, 1944 – during one of the Erie area's worst snowstorms. Luckily, the wedding was held just around the corner from the bride's home at Sacred Heart Church. In the photo above, you can see the procession of friends and relatives helping the bride travel through the snow to the church. Paul Canfield was a Marine serving in the South Pacific when he was wounded in Guam and sent to recover in a hospital in Buffalo. He came home to Erie for the ceremony and returned to Buffalo as soon as it was possible to leave Erie as all traveling was stopped for several days. After Paul's release from the Marine Corps, he went on to open the Canfield Auto Air Conditioner and Radiator Shop which is still in operation today (run by Paul and Irene's three sons) at 18th and State streets in Erie. *(Submitted by Irene Canfield).*

Presque Isle Ice-cycle

H.L. Kirk, a student at Gridley Junior High School in the mid-1940s, rides his bicycle out and around freighters that were frozen in Presque Isle Bay. *(Submitted by Harold Kirk).*

Washed ashore

Sophie Petroff rests on a life guard boat on one of Presque Isle's beaches in this 1940s photo. *(Submitted by Deborah Renner).*

Newly ordained

This photo depicts Father Scheffner celebrating his first mass after his ordination at his home parish of St. Boniface Church in 1943. Father Scheffner is shown, with his parents and two sisters, Marie and Helen Scheffner (in the back row). The girl in the front of the photo in the long gown was portraying the bride of Christ and the three girls behind her were carrying religious symbols: faith – a cross made of white roses; hope – an anchor made of pink roses; and, charity – a heart made of red roses (carried by Betty Krasnesky Twaroski). Father Scheffner served his first mass at his home parish of St. Boniface in 1943 and was the pastor at Mt. Carmel before his death. *(Submitted by Betty Krasnesky Twaroski).*

Scout's honor

Willie (Bray) Bruce shows off her new Girl Scout outfit in this 1949 photo. Founded in 1912 in Savannah, Georgia, by visionary Juliette Gordon Low, Girl Scouts started with a membership of only 18 girls and a dream. Juliette dreamed of giving the United States "something for all the girls." She envisioned an organization that would bring girls out of their cloistered home environments to serve in their communities and experience the open air. Within months, girl members were hiking through the woods in their knee-length blue uniforms, playing basketball in a curtained-off court, and going on camping trips. By 1920, Girl Scouts was growing in its independence, with its own uniform; its handbook, Scouting for Girls; and its own constitution and bylaws, contained in the Blue Book of Rules for Girl Scout Captains. *(Submitted Heather Cass, Willie's daughter).*

Quick dip
The Waidley family (l-r) Dorothy and Earle and their children (l-r) Joan Waidley Kelley and Bob Waidley spend a summer Sunday cooling off in Walnut Creek. *(Submitted by Bob Waidley).*

Long gone
The Eisert Building, at the corner of 6th and East Avenue, was built in 1914-15 by Frederick G. Eisert, right, a prominent east side businessman and owner of Eisert Hardware. Located on the first floor of the building (at different times) were: Eisert Hardware, Loblaw's grocery store, Adams & Struber Drug Store, a laundry and Dick's Variety. The second and third floors were all apartments. Eisert, a life-long   resident of Erie's first ward and a member of St. Ann's Church died in 1945 at the age of 75. The building was demolished the late 1960s to make way for a gas station which was then demolished when widening East Sixth Street for construction of the Bayfront Highway. *(Submitted by Ben Preston).*

Sigsbee house on the hill

The Sigsbee Reservoir house on West 26th Street is shown in this 1940s era photo. Fred Wittenburg was the caretaker of the house until his death in 1944. Fred and his wife, Hattie, raised five children at the house – Ruth, Margaret, Helen, Fritz and Harriet. (*Contributed by Virginia Kochanczyk and Eleanor Martin, granddaughters of Fred and Hattie*).

Erie industrious bayfront

As late as the 1950s, the Erie bayfront was a busy with ship traffic 24 hours a day, according to Lyman Cohen, who was in charge of personnel at the Erie Dock Company from 1941-1952. Cohen recalls that the ships would line up in the bay for as far as the eye could see. This photo of the P.E. Coal Dock shows a ship being loaded with coal. The iron structure on the dock was used to do the loading came through the Great Lakes upper peninsula and was loaded into railroad cars that would transport it to Sparrows Point, Md. for the Bethlehem Steel plants. According to Cohen, the men – a couple of hundred at the Erie Dock Co. – worked year-round loading and unloading ships and making repairs to the equipment throughout the winter. (*Submitted by Lyman Cohen*).

Teen Soldier

Joseph "Joe" Paris salutes the cameraman in this 1942 photo taken in the east side of Erie. Joe was just 16 years old when he enlisted in the United States Marine Corp and was sent to the South Pacific where he served in Okinawa and Iwo Jima during World War II. When he returned in 1945, he found employment as a butcher and married Mary Ann Waldemarson in 1926. They went on to have seven children: Kathleen, Thomas, Susan, Laura, Joseph, Timothy and William. (*Submitted by Tom Paris, son of Joe Paris*).

The Fabulous Fifties
1950-1959

The 1950s are remembered as America's idyllic period – a time of baseball and apple pie. Elvis invented Rock 'n roll, television invaded households and Erie celebrated 100 years of incorporation.

● Erie becomes the third largest city in Pennsylvania on June 1, 1950. Its population tops 130,125 a gain of 13,170 over the 1940 census, edging Scranton out of third place.

● Erie is divided into 10 postal zones to speed mail delivery on July 22, 1950. Residents have to learn to include a postal code on inter-city letters.

● The Erie Heights federal housing project nears completion. The $1.5 million subdivision includes 210 living units near 38th street and Taylor avenue.

● More than 100 firefighters battle a $2 million blaze on April 30, 1951, that guts the Twelfth Street Market after lightening hit the building. The building houses the Commodore Bowling alleys and the Twelfth Street Roller Skating Rink along with a variety of independent grocers, a restaurant and several small stores.

● Erie celebrates 100 years of incorporation with a parade in August of 1951.

● By the end of 1952, 17 million American homes have televisions, up from 7 million in 1950.

● Erie's reaction to the end of the Korean War in July of 1953 is met with much less fanfare than the announcement of the end of World War II just a few years before. In all, 52 Erie area men died serving the U.S. in the three-year Korean War.

● Ice traps several visitors on the peninsula until State Department plows and trucks open the ice-blocked roads of Presque Isle (1954).

● Elvis Presley launches Rock 'n Roll with his up-tempo version of blues tunes and nervous twitch of his leg (1954).

● WSEE celebrates its first birthday in 1955 as Erie's UHF television station and the local outlet for CBS.

● Polio vaccinations begin in the Erie schools (1955).

● Although the role of Erie's bayfront was shrinking, the summer of 1956, saw a great deal of activity, including iron ore. In 1959, the first ship through the St. Lawrence Seaway docked in Erie.

● The Erie Times Publishing Company acquires the Record Publishing Co. and begins offering the Morning News (1957).

● Mayor Arthur Gardner turns the first shovelful of dirt in the city's redevelopment area between Sassafras and Peach streets at 18th Street on Feb. 16, 1959.

● Construction is underway on Interstate 90 (1959).

● Fashion doll, Barbie, is born – March 9, 1959.

● Hawaii is admitted to the Union as the 50th State on Aug. 21, 1959.

Eight is NOT enough for the Longnecker "Family of the Year'

The 1953 "Family of the Year" – the Longneckers – are shown in front of St. Peter's Cathedral on Sassafras Street in Erie. The family included (l-r): Dolores (mother), Jon, Willard, Grover, Carole, Ellarie, Barbara, Edward, David, Gerard (father) and baby, Sandra Mae Longnecker. Two more children, Denise and Dennis, were born after this photo was taken. *(Submitted by Carole Longnecker Groters).*

Twin tennis titans

Cathedral Prep graduates and tennis stand-outs, twin brothers, Ed and Dick Koscelnik, were both awarded a four-year tennis scholarship to Duquesne University upon their high school graduation in 1950. The brothers also both married women named Patricia Ann. *(Submitted by Pat Koscelnik, wife of Ed).*

Fooling around at Freeport Beach

Dennis, 13, and Thomas, 10, Buto mug for the camera at their aunt Minnie Muscarella DiLoreto's beachfront cottage in North East about 1.5 miles east of Freeport Beach. The boys were the sons of Rose Muscarella Buto and her husband, Detective Sargent Nick Buto of the Erie Police force. *(Submitted by Loretta Muscarella Maurana, sister of Minnie and Rose Muscarella).*

A bigger fish to fry

The "Big Fish" Home Drive Inn was a prominent west side Erie landmark in the 1950s. *(Submitted by Paul Gaeckle).*

In photo: CO·K·ROSTER 4/6/53   3-1 · 3-2   FORT DEVENS, MASS. WHID·BOSTON

Soldiers ready for war

A group of Erie men pose for this 1953 photo at Fort Devens, Mass. before being sent to fight the Korean War. According to photo contributor, Frank Twaroski (second row from top, seventh man from left), Fort Devens was the Induction Center for these Army soldiers and was the last stop for these men before they were dispersed to different locations to fight the Korean War. *(Submitted by Frank Twaroski).*

Underwater dock?

Photographer, Ralph Carver captures Dobbins Landing, or the "Public Steamboat Landing" as it was called then, awash in waves during the winter storm that ravaged the bay in February of 1953. *(Submitted by Ralph Carver).*

Beautiful Bridle Path bridge

This c. 1949 photo taken by Ralph Carver shows the pond next to the Administration Building at the Peninsula now known as "Swan Cove." Ralph recalled that this was a popular spot for wedding party photos and a favorite place for photographers and artists. The bridge, which no longer exists, was known as the Bridle Path Bridge and was dedicated strictly for the use of horseback riders. At the time, visitors could rent horses at a stable on West Sixth Street and ride them through the park. *(Submitted by Ralph Carver).*

Maennerchor from before

It's unclear when this photo of the Maennerchor Music Hall (now known as the Erie Maennerchor Club) at 1607 State St. was taken, but it has a markedly different appearance today, with both turrets now gone. The original building committee when the Maennerchor was built in 1873 included Jacob Fritz, John Eberle, P. Heinrichs, George Gemunder, Carl Frank, C.A. Lang, Edward Hoffman, David Schlosser, Carl Prudenz, A.C. Vollmer and Charles Volland. *(Submitted by Beverly Pochatko).*

Get your goat – goat milk fudge that is!

Glenn J. Link poses with one of his goats in front of his goat milk fudge stand which was located on West Ridge Road in the 1950s. According to the photo contributor, the fudge stand attracted a lot of tourists and was primarily a retirement project for Mr. Link who owned a dairy goat farm. *(Submitted by Jean Leo Moore, granddaughter of Glenn Link).*

Bowling for teachers

The ladies pictured here are part of a teachers bowling league in Erie in the 1950s. Second from left is Molly Donaldson who taught fifth grade at Irving School. *(Submitted by Bob Weisenbach, Molly's nephew).*

Walking the beat

Erie City Police officer, Chester Wizikowski, walks by a "Erie Dispatch" paper box in this c. 1950s photo. Chester went on to become a Detective Sergeant in the Erie police force and had five children. *(Submitted by the grandchildren of Chester Wizikowski)*

Warsaw Cafe family

The Godzwa men – father, Ted, and sons, (l-r) Bob and Rick - pose outside the Warsaw Cafe at East 24th and Ash streets which was owned by Ted's parents, Anthony and Sophie Godzwa, when this 1953 photo was taken. Operation of the cafe was taken on by Anthony's son, Edwin and his wife, Helen Godzwa, in the late 1950s. Ted had two other sons that are not pictured here – Ted Jr. and Jim. *(Submitted by Rick Godzwa).*

The queen of popularity

In this photo, the 1950 "Popularity Queen," Jean Earickson, passes in front of Hossman Motor Sales in Girard during the Exchange Club Parade. Driving the 1950 Pontiac convertible carrying the queen and her court is Laura Hossman, wife of Earl Hossman who owned Hossman Motor Sales & Service on the corner of Main and Chestnut streets. *(Submitted by Earl Hossman).*

Chickens = Ticket Home

These chickens were the ticket to a trip back to her native Sweden for Amanda Peterson who kept the chickens at her West Third Street home. She sold the chickens' eggs and earned enough money to pay for the trip. Amanda and her husband, Hjalmar Peterson, had three sons. *(Submitted by Sheldon Peterson, grandson of Amanda Peterson).*

Ice to see you

The F. Buchner and Son Ice Company was located on East 21st Street and was owned by Fred Buchner, pictured in the far right of this c. 1950 photo. Fred and his son sold ice for use in ice boxes and the trucks shown here were used to deliver the ice to homes throughout the Erie area. Note the black "chutes" coming out of the building that were used to drop the ice into the waiting trucks. *(Submitted by Sharon Weed, daughter of Fred Buchner).*

Band in a shell

Mr. Anthony Savelli, shown in this 1950s era photo, directed concerts on Sunday afternoons in the Glenwood Park Bandshell. These free Sunday afternoon concerts were funded by the American Federation of Musicians and the Erie Parks Department. Many families came to enjoy their music each week. *(Submitted by Geraldine Oligeri, daughter of Anthony Savelli).*

Fuel for the big jobs

Pa. Gas Company (predecessor of National Fuel) workers take a break in front of their work trailer in this 1950s photo. The writing on the truck reads "Gas – for the Big Jobs – House Heating, Cooking, Refrigeration, Water Heating." In the photo at right, Pa. Gas Co. Mainline Foreman, William O. Hill Sr., surveys a jobsite. *(Submitted by Roger Hill, grandson of William O. Hill Sr.)*

Log unloader test-drive

This 1954 photo depicts the trial run of a Hydraulic Log Unloader using a Michigan Sling that was designed by Victor P. Mayer Sr. of Lawrence Park (in white hat). Victor was an Engineer at Hammermill Paper Co. and had previously worked at General Electric for about 10 years. *(Submitted by Elsie Mayer, wife of Victor).*

Monumental photo

The Perry Monument on Presque Isle State Park has long been the perfect place to gather with out-of-town relatives for a group photo as evidenced by this family in 1953. Pictured (l-r) are: Margaret Henley, Ruth Allen Ranson holding her infant daughter, Cathy Lyons, Bessie Daugherty, Dorothy Allen, John Allen and Geraldine Allen. When asked why they might have been so "dressed up," Ruth said that was just the way they dressed in those days and there was probably no particular reason they were in dresses and heels. Ruth and James Allen (not pictured) went on to have six children - Catharine, Charlene, Cheryl, Cassandra, James and Ernest. (Submitted by Ruth Allen Ranson).

Public Steamboat Landing

The Public Steamboat Landing, now known as Dobbins Landing, was a popular waterfront gathering spot for tourists and residents *(Submitted by Carol Saint)*.

Behrend's first

This 1948 photo depicts the first class (146 students) at Behrend College (now Penn State Erie, The Behrend College). When Penn State reorganized in 1959, the Commonwealth Campus System was established and The Behrend Center became The Behrend Campus of Penn State. Both the enrollments and the physical expanse of the campus grew throughout the 1960s and early '70s. By 1971, more than 1,200 students were enrolled. On Jan. 20, 1973, the Penn State Board of Trustees granted four-year college and graduate status to Penn State Erie. With that decision, Penn State Erie became the first Penn State location outside of University Park to achieve such status. Today, 3,700 students attend classes in original buildings from the Glenhill Farm Estate and in more recently constructed academic buildings. *(Submitted by the Office of Development and University Relations of Penn State Erie, The Behrend College).*

Come on in...the water's fine

This c. 1950s postcard depicts students enjoying the Behrend Center Pool at Behrend College (now Penn State Erie, The Behrend College) on Station Road in Harborcreek township. *(Submitted by the Office of Development and University Relations of Penn State Erie, The Behrend College).*

SWIMMING POOL
BEHREND CENTER
ERIE, PA.

Radio flyer riders
Sisters Karen and Linda Church wait for someone to give them a ride in their Radio Flyer wagon in their grandparents' yard on Homer Avenue in 1950. The girls are the daughters of Amos and Ruth Church. *(Submitted by Karen Clement).*

Behrend's beginnings
Students relax in front of the Glenhill Farmhouse at Behrend Center (now Penn State Erie, The Behrend College) in this 1950s shot. The college's campus was donated to the University in 1948 by Mary Behrend in memory of her husband, Ernst, co-founder (with his father and brother) of the Hammermill Paper Company. In donating her family's Glenhill Farm Estate to Penn State, Mrs. Behrend was responding to the need, expressed by a committee of prominent Erie residents, for a public, co-education, non-sectarian university presence in Erie. *(Submitted by the Office of Development and University Relations of Penn State Erie, The Behrend College).*

Harborcreek's Central School

Students in Mrs. Francis Luellen's first grade class pose for this 1956 photo at Central School in Harborcreek. Organized in 1803 as one of the original 16 townships of Erie county, Harborcreek had a population of 70 to 100 people but soon became one of the wealthiest and most populous communities in Erie County. Many of the roads, creeks, and one-room school houses were named for the early settlers and there are descendants of these families still living in the township. *(Donated to the Harborcreek Historical Society by Carol Laughlin).*

East High gridiron warriors

The East High School 1951 football team is pictured in this snapshot. (*Submitted by Linda Evans, daughter of Richard Pletz, first row, far right*).

Clowning classmates

East High School classmates, Alice Beresowski, Beryl Hodges, Jane Gatti and Elaine Dixon (on knees) clown around in this 1953 photo taken in Perry Square. Notice the buildings in the background on the northeast corner of Sixth and French streets (where Erie Insurance now stands). The fountain, directly behind the girls, still stands. All but one of the ladies pictured here live in the Erie area. (*Submitted by Jane Gatti Hubiak*).

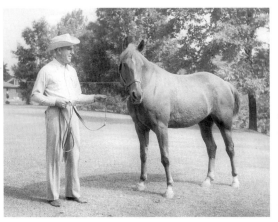

Stormy's successful reign

The horse shown in this 1956 photo is "Mac's Stormy" affectionately called "Stormy" by his owner, Earl Hossman (holding horse). Stormy was a registered quarterhorse gelding and grand champion in Michigan, Ohio and Pennsylvania in 1959. He was ridden in this class in Newark, Ohio, fairgrounds by Dale Wilkinson and was first out of 15 entries. (*Submitted by Earl Hossman*).

Where business careers begin

Erie Business Center opened its doors in 1884 as Clark's Business College and quickly became one of the foremost business training institutions in our part of the country. In 1932, Charles P. McGeary, Sr. became owner and president of what was then known as Erie Business College. He continued to direct the school until his death in 1953. His wife, Chelsie S. McGeary, then assumed the presidency of the institution until her death in 1972. Charles P. McGeary, Jr. took over as Director, a position he held until 1988. Today, Mr. McGeary serves as president and chairman of the board of directors with his wife, Hope A. McGeary, serving as Vice President and Secretary of the Board. *(Submitted by the Erie Business Center)*.

Garfield second graders

The second grade at Garfield School, once located at 21st and German streets in Erie, pose for a class picture in this 1956 photo. The teacher, Mrs. Bukowska, is pictured in the top row at the far right. Students in the photo include (in no particular order): Monica Gambill (photo contributor – first row, second from right), Charles Strickland, Barry Baker, Harry Johnson, Carol Williams, Peggy Jordan, Karen Bryant, Marlene Harris, JoAnn Spencer, James Hollingsworth, Oscar Hursh and Q. Beason. *(Submitted by Monica Gambill Pullium).*

A softer sidewalk

Gertrude Baumann Lacey and Myrtle Flaherty try out the first outdoor carpet in front of Baumann Brothers carpet in June of 1950. George Baumann looks on from the doorway of the store's original, 644 E. 5th St. store, which has been in business in Erie since the 1800s. *(Submitted by Baumann Bros. CarpeTowne, now located at 1404 E. 12th St.)*

Three of a kind

All three of these young ladies hailed from Oil City, attended Hamot School of Nursing (from which they graduated in 1951) and all three married men from Erie who went to school together. The women are: (l-r) Patricia Downs Honard, JoAnne Dunlap Carey and Betty Ann Evans Hellwege. This photo was taken in 1950, one year before they graduated from nursing school. *(Submitted by Kathleen Carey Longley, JoAnne's daughter).*

Creek car wash

This photo shows a group of teens washing their car in a North East creek in 1955. That's one way to conserve water! *(Submitted by Mary Wheaton).*

Just for men

The Robert Hall Clothes store was located on East 26th Street, just east of Parade Street (where Hoffman's Religious Goods is now located) and sold fine men's clothing. Shown here are exterior and interior photos of the store taken about 1952. Robert Hall had a second location on West 26th Street as well. *(Submitted by Gary Mazzocco whose father, Gilbert Mazzocco Sr., managed the East 26th Street store).*

Second to none

The Second Baptist Church, in its original location at 124 E. 18th St., is depicted at left in this 1950s era photo. Below is the church's pastor at the time this photo was taken, Reverend A.H. Hunter, and his wife, Josephine. The Second Baptist Church has occupied several locations since this photo was taken including East Eighth Street and 32nd and Tuttle streets, before settling at its current location of 26th and Wayne streets in Erie. (Submitted by Monica Pullium).

Golden Girl on Erie's stage

Shown here is a scene from the Erie Playhouse's mid-1950s performance of "The Desk Set." The actors are: (l-r) Edward Hamilton, Rue McClanahan (of "Golden Girls" fame), Natalie Ross, Jean Tarrant (widow of the late Newell Tarrant, director of the theatre in those days) and Margaret Laver. This photo was taken when the Erie Playhouse was located at 128 W. 7th St. *(Submitted by Betty Peebles).*

Old Wesleyville Baptist Church

This photo shows the old Wesleyville Baptist Church which was located on the corner of South and Center streets. The church, founded in 1893, is currently located on the corner of Market Street and Buffalo Road where it was built in 1973. *(Submitted by Willie Bray Bruce).*

The growth of Griswold

The Griswold Manufacturing Company's float (which reads "Born in Erie, Growing with Erie – 1865-1951) is shown in this 1951 parade photo. In 1865, two Erie families associated by marriage, joined in a modest venture to manufacture door hinges. The Selden and Griswold union paved the way for The Griswold Manufacturing Company of Erie, Pa., recognized world wide as producers of fine cast iron products, especially cookware. Between 1865 and 1957, when they closed production of the plant at the corner of 12th and Raspberry streets, their line of cookware had been sold and used around the world. Their designers and engineers produced many patents spanning almost 100 years of manufacturing. Before the turn of the 20th century, they added cast aluminum products to their line. In the 1920s they enameled some cookware and by the 1930s they offered electric items to their product list. They also produced commercial pieces for use in restaurants. *(Submitted by Scott Mealy).*

Ride 'em cowgirl!

Monica Gambill, 5, poses for this 1950s cowgirl photo outside her family home on East 18th Street. The pony belonged to the photographer who would take the pony and cowboy clothes, door-to-door, selling parents the opportunity to have their child photographed on the pony. *(Submitted by Monica Gambill Pullium).*

Cooking up a new 'do in the kitchen

Genevieve Murphy gives her daughter, Patricia, a "Toni Home Perm" in the kitchen of their Hastings Road home. Genevieve was an RN at Saint Vincent's Hospital where her daughter, Patricia, later came to work as a Labor and Delivery Nurse. *(Submitted by Patricia Murphy).*

Beach baby

Cheryl (Mack) Goetz plays in the sand at Presque Isle in this 1959 snapshot. *(Submitted by Cheryl Goetz).*

Reunited band of brothers

Dan and Clarabell Munson's family held a joyous reunion in December of 1945 when their three sons returned home after serving in World War II. Pictured, l-r, are Ken (Kenneth), Clarabell, Jerry (Gerald), Dan and Del (Delbert). During the war, Ken was stationed in Tehran, Iran, with the Transportation Corps; Jerry was a member of a B-29 bomber crew that flew bombing missions over Japan; and, Del was a radar communications specialist in the European theater. *(Submitted by Libby Munson-Kramer, Jerry's wife).*

137

The Swingin' Sixties
1960-1969

The 1960s were one of the most turbulent times in America's history and Erie was no exception. From the fight for racial equality to war protests to the construction of new buildings and schools – the Erie area saw its fair share of change during this tumultuous decade.

● John F. Kennedy visits Erie on Sept. 28, 1960 on a presidential campaign stop. He stood on the south side of the Lawrence Hotel and spoke, leaving an indelible impression on the thousands who gathered to hear him speak.

● In the mid 1960s, the old Lawrence Hotel at 10th and Peach streets was razed to make way for the Erie Hilton.

● Erie residents gathered wherever there was a radio or television set to experience the last few moments of the final countdown of the flight of astronaut John Glenn in 1962.

● The Erie Zoological Society opens an ice rink at 38th and Cherry streets next door to the zoo that will provide ice skating for the public for a nominal fee that benefits the zoo (1962).

● Restoration of the Brig Niagara continues as crews work to raise the masts onto the ship (1963).

● On Nov. 22, 1963, all of Erie mourns the death of President John F. Kennedy.

● The Beatles, a Liverpool pop group, causes the most raucous British invasion since the War of 1812, when they arrive on U.S. soil on Feb. 7, 1964.

● The Millcreek Township School District constructs the Chestnut Hill Elementary School at 54th and Clinton streets at a cost of $750,000 (1965).

● A fire destroys the Second Baptist Church, 125 E. 8th St., on Feb. 1, 1965. More than 100 firefighters fight the flames in sub-zero temperatures. The damage is estimated at $175,000.

● Pennsylvania approves the proposed Bayfront Highway (1965).

● Lou Tullio lost the 1965 Democratic primary for Erie Mayor to Mike Cannavino. But, when Cannavino suffered a heart attack, Tullio took his spot on the ticket and defeated incumbent Mayor Charles Williamson by 3,000 votes – the narrowest victory margin of his six elections. He would remain in office for 24 years.

● Black business leaders in Erie submit a request to Mayor Tullio, asking for $40,000 to reactivate the Booker T. Washington Center in 1967.

● The old Tech High School on 10th and Sassafras streets is sold to the Erie Dioceses for $250,000. The building now houses the Cathedral Center.

● The Reverend Martin Luther King Jr., a prophet of nonviolence and racial brotherhood, is gunned down on April 4, 1968 at a Memphis hotel. Less than two months after King's slaying, Sen. Robert F. Kennedy is shot in the head in Los Angeles early June 5 after winning the Ca. primary in his quest for the Democratic presidential nomination.

● Edinboro's Normal Hall, a landmark 108-year-old building on the Edinboro State College campus, is destroyed in by fire on May 14, 1969. The building held all the records and files of past and present students.

● The Woodstock Music and Art Fair is held during the long weekend of Aug. 15-18 in a field near Bethel, NY in 1969.

JFK in Erie

John F. Kennedy smiles for photographers in this October 1960 photo taken in downtown Erie. Erie City Police officer, Chester Wizikowski, (in hat directly behind Kennedy) helped to provide security for JFK while he was in town on a campaign stop. He spoke on the steps of the Lawrence Hotel. *(Submitted by the grandchildren of Chester Wizikowski).*

Kennedy memorial campaign

Following the assassination of President John F. Kennedy, Erie city councilman, Bernard "Babe" Harkins organized a fundraising campaign to create a Kennedy Memorial in Erie City Hall. In the photo above, Babe (far right) poses with Huck and Sis Linenger in this fundraising photo opportunity taken poolside at the Linenger residence. In the photo above right, Babe poses with some of the children who helped with the fundraising effort and at, right, is the Kennedy Memorial that was dedicated in Erie City Hall on May 28, 1965. (Submitted by Pat Harkins, Babe's son).

Huckleberry Finn revisited?

This homemade raft was built by Jerry Cornell and Al Waller and always created lots of excitement in western Erie county in the early 1960s. Here it is shown at the mouth of Elk Creek in Lake City prior to entering Lake Erie. Those on board include: Bob and Mary Bowen, Clancy Hanzelka, Dale Miller, "Hammer" Andrews, "Smokey" Hanson, Barb Cornell and Jack Waller (foreground). The vessel perished during a summer storm in 1964 while moored. *(Submitted by Robert B. Martin).*

Summer of '63 stroll

Barbara Ann Korn takes her firstborn son, David, for a stroller ride in the 1400 block of Lynn Street during the summer of 1963. Note the netting over the buggy that kept insects away from the baby. *(Submitted by David W. Korn)*

Drink up, Bubbles!

Everyone who is old enough to have visited the Erie Zoo in the 1960s remembers "Bubbles" the beloved Erie Zoo elephant shown here in this 1964 photo. The baby elephant was donated by the Security Peoples Trust Co. and was much loved by zoo visitors of all ages. In this photo, Bubbles is fed a bottle of milk in the children's zoo (then known as "Pixieland") while some unidentified children look on. *(Photo submitted by the Erie Zoological Society).*

Humpty Dumpty sat on a wall
This Humpty Dumpty sat on a wall in "Pixieland" (later renamed the Children's Zoo) at the Erie Zoo in the 1960s. Pixieland featured brightly painted buildings, fences and areas just for the children to play and was a favorite place of Erie area children in the 60s. *(Submitted by the Erie Zoological Society).*

Playtime in Pixie Land
Pixieland was, by far, the most popular area of the Erie Zoo with the children of the '60s and '70s. In the photo above, children, John Willow (on donkey) and Julie Mertens pose in front of the Pixieland sign on opening day – June 30, 1963. In the photo at right are two Pixieland animal attendants dressed in their Pixieland costumes, complete with bells on their shoes. The area was later renovated and renamed the "Children's Zoo" and is currently undergoing a second major renovation expected to be completed in 2004. *(Submitted by the Erie Zoological Society).*

St. Michael's fire

St. Michael's Catholic Church, 621 W. 17th St., is shown at the left before fire destroyed the church in the 1970s (above). Built in 1883, St. Michael's originally served one of the city's German neighborhoods and was established under Rev. James Lachermaier, founding pastor of St. Michael's. The interior of the church was distinguished by massive oak panels and pews. The rectory was attached to the church and nearby was the convent. St. Michael's served the community until Nov. 10, 1973 when a fire originating in the basement of the attached rectory destroyed the historic church and rectory. The pastor, Msgr. Edward Latimer and assistants, Fr. Vincent Enright and Fr. Gerald Koos, barely escaped the fiery disaster. It was decided to raze the church rather than rebuild for several reasons – the financial cost of rebuilding the church, the deteriorating neighborhood and the proximity of nearby St. Paul's Church at 16th and Walnut streets. *(Submitted by Beverly Pochatko).*

Beachcomber Buffet

A buffet is being served at the Beachcomber Hotel on the opening night of the Erie Playhouse's Peninsula Summer Tent Theatre in 1961. At right, is Bob Majeroni, owner of the popular hotel. The tent theatre and hotel/restaurant were located on the peninsula across from where Joe Roots Grill is now located. At left, in the forefront, is Herta Kilpatrick. *(Submitted by Betty Peebles).*

Alice in Erieland

Erie native, Ann B. Davis, relaxes at home in Erie with her dog Byon in this 1950s photo taken between her starring appearances in the "Bob Cummings Show" and (later) the "Brady Bunch. While she lived in Erie, Ann appeared in many Erie Playhouse shows and later, starred on Broadway in "Once Upon a Mattress." Ann is now semi-retired and living in Texas and still performs a bit of theatre. *(Submitted by Betty Peebles).*

Mush!

The Arctic sled dog races were a big hit at Erie's first Winter Carnival in 1963. In the background, at left, is the late Dave Forsythe, a popular WICU-TV news announcer who chaired the "sled dogs" event. *(Submitted by Betty Peebles).*

Winter carnival royal family

Three key players in Erie's first Winter Carnival are pictured in this 1963 photo. At left is Mark Wargo, former Park Operations Manager at Presque Isle State Park, who was in charge of fireworks at the winter carnival; Carnival Queen, the former Sue Peterman ("Miss Erie" at the time); and Carnival King, Jim Cross. *(Submitted by Betty Peebles).*

Future hall-of-famer at work

Pictured here is Al Bonnell, an engine mechanic and a well-known Erie race car driver, at work at the Poplar White Truck Company on West 12th Street. This photo, taken in 1963 shows Al in the company's pump room working on rebuilding a fuel pump. Al was recently elected to the National Auto Racing Hall of Fame after a 20-year career that ended in 1949. He was the most popular midget car driver in the nation in the 1940s. *(Submitted by Jennifer Durst Manno, president of Poplar Parks & Service).*

Brig on land

Nancy Regruth Latimer poses next to the Brig Niagara in this early 1960s photo taken at Dobbins Landing in Erie. During that time, the Niagara was no longer in the water, but was up on blocks on land. It would be many years before the Niagara was restored and able to sail once again. *(Submitted by Nancy Latimer).*

Meet me under the clock

Pictured here are the "Special" tables on the main floor of the Boston Store on State Street in downtown Erie. The Boston Store's origins go back to 1885, when the Erie Dry Goods Co. was purchased by Elisha H. Mack. Under the direction of the young New York man, the store soon began to grow. Mack decided to give his store a new name. At the time, the city of Boston, Ma. was a renowned center of European fashion and culture. To denote their superior quality of merchandise, the Erie Dry Goods Co. adopted the name "Boston Store." The store's new name promised the latest of fashion trends and the Boston Store carried complete lines of the newest merchandise available. A year later, in 1886, the Boston Store moved to a slightly larger store front in the Olds Building at 718 State St. Now in the center of Erie, the store promptly became a popular place to shop. Eventually, the Boston Store gained frontage on Peach, Seventh, and Eighth streets. These buildings were all demolished to make way for a modern six story structure, creating Erie's largest department store. The Boston Store's size and many features distinguished it from every other store in Erie. Perhaps no other feature is as well remembered as the Boston Store clock. The familiar Erie phrase "I'll meet you under the clock" was used when one would meet a friend downtown. The large, bronze clock (as seen in this photo) was centrally located on the Boston Store's main floor. *(Submitted by John Baker, history provided by Mike Monroe).*

Blueprint for success

Rectenwald Blueprint & Supply Co., founded in 1960 by Norb Rectenwald, is a blueprint reproduction and supply house that works with all types of draftspeople, engineers, contractors and architects in the Erie area. In the 1960s, Rectenwald Blueprint was located at Sixth and French streets (where the white columns in front of Erie Insurance now stand). The line-up on that corner, as pictured above, included the Perry Square Cafe on the left, the ECDAP (Erie County Drug Abuse) Outreach Center on the right and Lakes Electric and Zink's Dry Cleaners further down the block (not pictured). *(Submitted by Warren Vollbrecht of the Rectenwald Blueprint & Supply Co.)*

All aboard!

In this 1969 photo, locomotive engineer, John Szympruch Jr., hauls an oversized boiler from the Erie City Iron Works, which was located at 12th and East avenue, (now owned by Zurn Industries) to Cleveland on a NY Central System locomotive. John is still an engineer today as was his father, John Sr., before him. *(Submitted by John Szympruch).*

INDEX